BUSINESS CALCULATIONS

Business Calculations
Second Edition

K. R. Bishop
BSc.Econ.(Hons), ACP, FRSA
Principal, East Ham College of Technology
Former Chief Examiner to the Business Education Council in Business
Calculations

Holt, Rinehart and Winston
London· New York · Sydney · Toronto

Holt, Rinehart and Winston Ltd: 1 St Anne's Road,
Eastbourne, East Sussex BN21 3UN

British Library Cataloguing in Publication Data

Bishop, K. R.
   Business calculations — 2nd ed.
   1. Business mathematics
   I. Title
   513′.93   HF5691

ISBN 0-03-910537-7

First published by Cassell Ltd 1979
Second edition 1984

Last digit is print no: 9 8 7 6 5 4 3 2 1

Printed in Great Britain by Billing & Sons, Worcester

Contents

Preface

This second edition of *Business Calculations* has been updated and completely revised in accordance with the new specification for the BTEC General Award. Part I covers the general objectives of the module, with test papers at the end of each section. Part II covers the main applications of Business Calculations, with examples and suggested assignments for students to undertake. This part of the book is arranged under topic headings. It is not anticipated that all students will cover all sections. This depends on the special interests of the students, or the particular type of employment in which they are engaged.

The new BTEC General Award emphasises the need for students to be made aware of the impact of new technology in business, and the Business Calculations module refers specifically to the use of electronic calculators and computers. In the same way that calculators have simplified arithmetical computation, the development of computers has increased the speed and efficiency of carrying out a vast range of business functions.

Students are expected to use calculators, wherever appropriate, throughout the course, and reference is made to this in Section C. Students are also expected to have some practical experience in using computers. There are a number of business areas, e.g. preparation of payroll details, processing of orders and issuing invoices – all involving calculations – in which computers are now commonly used. These topics also provide students with good practical examples of how to relate numerical skills to a business context.

K.R.B.

Part I

A. The four basic rules of arithmetic

1. Addition and Subtraction

Exercise A1

1. The following tables gives the monthly sales for the departments of a small store. Add the columns vertically and horizontally and check the final total in the space marked Grand Total.

Dept	Jan	Feb	Mar	Total
	£	£	£	£
A	13 320	12 490	12 960	
B	8 560	6 998	7 234	
C	7 856	7 623	8 001	
D	5 239	5 146	6 114	
					←Grand Total

2. The following table shows the consumption in therms and the cost of gas over a period of two years. Complete the table, indicating an increase by + and a decrease by −.

Quarter	1982 Gas consumed	Cost (£)	1983 Gas consumed	Cost (£)	Increase or decrease Consumption	Cost (£)
1	446·4	145·15	491·2	174·45		
2	336·6	111·66	289·8	106·98		
3	95·6	38·16	190·2	73·61		
4	196·3	68·87	45·8	25·24		

3.   The following table gives the cost prices and selling prices of a number of items. Calculate the profit on each item and complete the table by totalling the three columns. Check the total profit figure.

Item	Selling Price (S.P.) £	Cost Price (C.P.) £	Profit (S.P.−C.P.) £
A	13·83	10·45	
B	16·45	12·13	
C	14·00	9·64	
D	19·24	15·30	
E	32.53	26·74	
F	29·92	24·08	
G	24·64	19·89	
Totals			

4.   Complete the following table which summarises the weekly sales for a number of salesmen.

Salesman	Cash sales (£)	Credit sales (£)	Total
Smith	56·45	494·32	
Brown	64·03	576·20	
James	41·10	352·12	
Bond	74·92	619·79	
Wilson	59·15	515·24	
Totals			

5.   The following is a summary of the receipts and payments of a club for one year. Complete the account and calculate the balance in hand.

Receipts (£)		Payments (£)
137·00		56·24
24·56		25·42
45·00		70·00
9·50		4·50
17·25		
11·24	*Balance*	

6.   Complete and balance the following account:

Receipts (£)	Payments (£)
149·00	136·00
24·35	24·50
46·50	27·39
1·25	104·53
12·72	
113·24	
54·22	

2.   Multiplication

Example   (i) $246 \times 43 =$

$$
\begin{array}{r}
246 \\
43 \\
\hline
\end{array}
$$

$$(246 \times \ 3) = 738$$
$$(246 \times 40) = 9\ 840$$

$$10\ 578$$

Example   (ii) $389 \times 49 = (389 \times 50) - (389 \times 1)$
$$= \quad 19\,450 \quad - \quad 389$$
$$= \qquad\qquad 19\,061$$

Example   (iii) $274 \times 25 = 274 \times \dfrac{100}{4}$
$$= \dfrac{27\,400}{4}$$
$$= 6\,850$$

Exercise A2

Using the simplest method you know, calculate the following:

1. 147×12
2. 3049×63
3. 744×25
4. 596×199
5. 833×2700

6. 564×125
7. 124×101
8. 2013×37
9. 901×79
10. 840×48

3. Division

Example   (i) $3987 \div 34 \quad = \qquad\qquad 117$

$\qquad\qquad\qquad\qquad\qquad\qquad\quad 34)\overline{3987}$

$\qquad\qquad\qquad = 117 \text{ Rem } 9 \qquad\quad \underline{34}$

$\qquad\qquad\qquad\qquad\qquad\qquad\qquad\qquad 58$

$\qquad\qquad\qquad\qquad\qquad\qquad\qquad\quad \underline{34}$

$\qquad\qquad\qquad\qquad\qquad\qquad\qquad 247$

$\qquad\qquad\qquad\qquad\qquad\qquad\qquad \underline{238}$

$\qquad\qquad\qquad\qquad\qquad\qquad\qquad\qquad 9 \text{ Rem.}$

Example   (ii) $7812 \div 63 \quad = \qquad 9)\overline{7812}$

$\qquad\qquad\qquad = 7812 \div (9 \times 7) \qquad 7)\ \overline{\ 868}$

$\qquad\qquad\qquad = \quad 124 \qquad\qquad\qquad\quad \overline{124}$

Exercise A3

Using the simplest method you know, calculate the following:

1. $3177 \div 9$
2. $7468 \div 23$
3. $875 \div 25$
4. $4032 \div 72$
5. $849\,000 \div 300$

6. $8129 \div 37$
7. $7462 \div 151$
8. $4000 \div 125$
9. $6954 \div 121$
10. $1000 \div 365$

4. Factors, Indices, HCF and LCM

4.1 Factors

Example
$$30 = 1 \times 30$$
$$30 = 1 \times 2 \times 15$$
$$30 = 1 \times 2 \times 3 \times 5$$

We say that 1, 2, 3 and 5 are the Prime Factors of 30, i.e. factors which are all Prime Numbers.

A Prime Number is a number which has no factors other than itself and 1, e.g. 5, 7, 11 and 13.

4.2 Indices

When factorised a number may be more conveniently written in Index form.

Example
$$4 = 2 \times 2 \qquad = 2^2$$
$$8 = 2 \times 2 \times 2 \qquad = 2^3$$
$$16 = 2 \times 2 \times 2 \times 2 = 2^4$$

The small numbers 2, 3 and 4 are Index numbers.

Example
$$600 = 2 \times 2 \times 2 \times 3 \times 5 \times 5$$
$$= \underline{\underline{2^3 \times 3 \times 5^2}} \qquad \text{expressed in index form.}$$

4.3 HCF and LCM

The Highest Common Factor (HCF) of two numbers is the largest number which will divide exactly into each of them.

The Lowest Common Multiple (LCM) of two numbers is the smallest of which both are factors.

Example
$$24 = 2 \times 2 \times 2 \times 3$$
$$30 = \phantom{2 \times{}} 2 \times 3 \times 5$$
$$\text{HCF} = \phantom{2 \times 2 \times{}} 2 \times 3 = 6$$

$$\text{LCM} = 2 \times 2 \times 2 \times 3 \times 5 = 120$$

Exercise A4

Express the following in Prime Factors in Index form:

1. 81	3. 124	5. 480	7. 4428
2. 99	4. 369	6. 513	8. 79 800

Find the HCF of the following sets of numbers:

9. 30, 48	11. 70, 98, 112	13. 144, 378, 900
10. 30, 60, 105	12. 76, 95, 228	14. 210, 630, 2700

Find the LCM of the following sets of numbers:

15. 4, 8, 10	17. 6, 16, 20	19. 16, 24, 36
16. 3, 5, 16	18. 12, 18, 20	20. 40, 64, 96

5.   Fractions

5.1   Definitions

A fraction is expressed as one number divided by another, e.g. $\frac{1}{2}$, $\frac{2}{3}$, $\frac{3}{5}$. The top number is called the Numerator and the bottom number the Denominator. The denominator indicates the number of parts into which the whole quantity has been divided and the numerator the number of these parts making up the fraction.

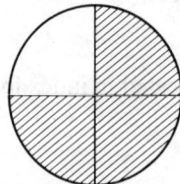

In the diagram the circle has been divided into 4 equal parts, of which 3 are shaded. The shaded portion therefore represents $\frac{3}{4}$ of the whole circle.

Fractions of equal value can be written in a number of ways.

Example $\frac{1}{2} = \frac{2}{4} = \frac{3}{6} = \frac{5}{10}$ etc.

Fractions can also be simplified if the numerator and denominator can be divided by the same number.

Example　　　　　(i) $\frac{15}{18} = \frac{5}{6}$ (dividing by 3)

　　　　　　　　　(ii) $\frac{18}{20} = \frac{9}{10}$ (dividing by 2)

This is known as reducing fractions to their Lowest Terms.

A Proper Fraction is a fraction where the numerator is smaller than the denominator, e.g. $\frac{4}{5}$ or $\frac{3}{8}$.

An Improper Fraction is a fraction where the numerator is greater than the denominator, e.g. $\frac{4}{3}$ or $\frac{15}{4}$.

A Mixed Number is a fraction comprising a whole number and a proper fraction, e.g. $1\frac{1}{2}$ or $3\frac{5}{6}$. Improper fractions can also be written as mixed numbers, e.g. $\frac{4}{3} = 1\frac{1}{3}$ and $\frac{15}{4} = 3\frac{3}{4}$.

5.2　Addition and Subtraction

To add or subtract fractions they must first have the same denominators.

Example　　(i) $\frac{1}{5} + \frac{3}{5} = \frac{4}{5}$　　(ii) $\frac{7}{10} - \frac{3}{10} = \frac{4}{10} = \frac{2}{5}$.

If the fractions have different denominators they must be converted to equivalent fractions with the same denominators.

Example　　　　　(i) $\frac{1}{3} + \frac{1}{2} = \frac{2}{6} + \frac{3}{6} = \frac{5}{6}$.

　　　　　　　　　(ii) $\frac{3}{4} + \frac{2}{5} = \frac{15}{20} + \frac{8}{20} = \frac{23}{20} = 1\frac{3}{20}$.

This means finding the LCM of the denominators.

Example　　　　(i)　　$\frac{1}{2} + \frac{3}{4} - \frac{2}{3}$　(LCM = 12)

　　　　　　　　　　　$= \frac{6}{12} + \frac{9}{12} - \frac{8}{12} = \frac{7}{12}$.

Example　　　　(ii)　　$2\frac{2}{3} + 4\frac{1}{5} - 1\frac{1}{2}$　(LCM = 30)

　　　　　　　　　　　$= 2\frac{20}{30} + 4\frac{6}{30} - 1\frac{15}{30}$

　　　　　　　　　　　$= 5\,\frac{20+6-15}{30}$

　　　　　　　　　　　$= 5\frac{11}{30}$

Example   (iii) $5\frac{3}{8}-2\frac{2}{3}$ (LCM = 24)

$$= 3\,\frac{9-16}{24}$$

$$= 2\,\frac{24+9-16}{24}$$ To make fraction positive reduce whole number by 1 and change the 1 to $\frac{24}{24}$.

$$= 2\,\frac{33-16}{24}\quad = 2\frac{17}{24}.$$

5.3   Multiplication

Multiplying fractions together requires the multiplication of the numerators and the multiplication of the denominators. This can be illustrated as follows:

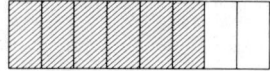

$\frac{3}{4}$ of the whole $= \frac{6}{8}$ (the shaded portion)

$\frac{1}{2}$ of $\frac{3}{4} = \frac{3}{8}$ (the shaded portion)

Examples   (i) $\frac{1}{2}$ of $\frac{3}{4} = \frac{1}{2}\times\frac{3}{4} = \frac{3}{8}$

(ii) $\frac{2}{3}$ of $\frac{4}{5} = \frac{2}{3}\times\frac{4}{5} = \frac{8}{15}.$

If a numerator and denominator have a common factor then this can be cancelled out before multiplying.

Example $\frac{3}{4}\times\frac{3}{5}\times\frac{5}{6} = \dfrac{3\times1\times1}{4\times1\times2} = \frac{3}{8}.$

Where fractions are mixed numbers they must first be changed to improper fractions before multiplying.

Example $4\frac{1}{2}\times1\frac{2}{3} = \frac{9}{2}\times\frac{5}{3}$

$$= \frac{3}{2}\times\frac{5}{1} = \frac{15}{2} = 7\frac{1}{2}.$$

5.4   Division

The rule for division is to invert the divisor and multiply. Mixed numbers must first be changed to improper fractions. This can be illustrated as follows:

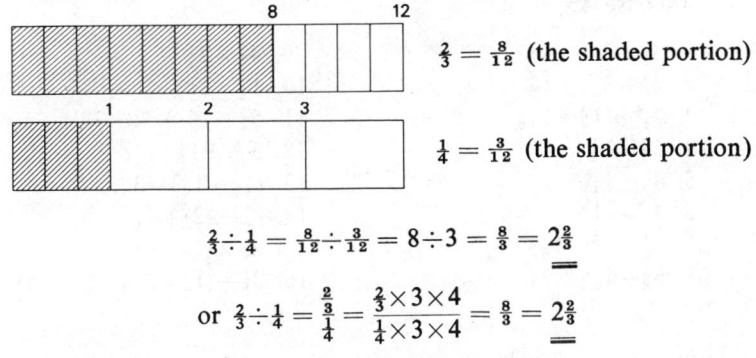

$\frac{2}{3} = \frac{8}{12}$ (the shaded portion)

$\frac{1}{4} = \frac{3}{12}$ (the shaded portion)

$$\tfrac{2}{3} \div \tfrac{1}{4} = \tfrac{8}{12} \div \tfrac{3}{12} = 8 \div 3 = \tfrac{8}{3} = 2\tfrac{2}{3}$$

$$\text{or } \tfrac{2}{3} \div \tfrac{1}{4} = \frac{\frac{2}{3}}{\frac{1}{4}} = \frac{\frac{2}{3} \times 3 \times 4}{\frac{1}{4} \times 3 \times 4} = \tfrac{8}{3} = 2\tfrac{2}{3}$$

It will be seen, therefore, that when we divide fractions we need to have the two fractions expressed with the same denominators. Inverting the divisor and multiplying is a simple way to achieve this.

Example

(i) $\frac{6}{1} \div \frac{3}{1} = \frac{6}{1} \times \frac{1}{3} = \frac{6}{3} = 2.$

(ii) $\frac{3}{4} \div \frac{1}{4} = \frac{3}{4} \times \frac{4}{1} = \frac{3}{1} = 3.$

(iii) $\frac{4}{5} \div \frac{3}{10} = \frac{4}{5} \times \frac{10}{3} = \frac{8}{3} = 2\frac{2}{3}.$

(iv) $3\frac{3}{4} \div 1\frac{1}{8} = \frac{15}{4} \div \frac{9}{8} \qquad = \frac{15}{4} \times \frac{8}{9}$
$\qquad = \frac{10}{3} = 3\frac{1}{3}.$

5.5 Brackets

Sometimes a problem involves several operations. This can be confusing unless brackets are used to make the order of operation clear.

Take the example $2+3\times4$

This could mean $(2+3)\times4 = 5\times4 = 20$
or $2+(3\times4) = 2+12 = 14$

By using brackets we indicate which part must be worked first.

Example $(4\frac{1}{2} \div 2) + 1\frac{3}{4} - (1\frac{1}{8} \times \frac{1}{3})$
$= \quad 2\frac{1}{4} \quad + 1\frac{3}{4} - \quad \frac{3}{8}$
$= 3\frac{2+6-3}{8} = 3\frac{5}{8}.$

Exercise A5

1. $3\frac{1}{8}+2\frac{5}{16}+1\frac{1}{4}$
2. $4\frac{1}{5}+3\frac{7}{10}+1\frac{1}{2}$
3. $2\frac{5}{12}+1\frac{3}{4}+1\frac{11}{16}$
4. $5\frac{3}{4}-1\frac{1}{8}$
5. $4\frac{1}{2}-1\frac{7}{12}$
6. $4\frac{3}{10}-1\frac{3}{5}$
7. $5\frac{1}{2}+1\frac{3}{4}-1\frac{1}{8}$
8. $6\frac{3}{8}-1\frac{9}{16}+2\frac{1}{2}$

9. $4\frac{1}{4}\times3\frac{1}{2}$
10. $1\frac{3}{8}\times2\frac{2}{3}$
11. $5\frac{3}{4}\div1\frac{5}{8}$
12. $3\frac{5}{12}+1\frac{1}{8}$
13. $(1\frac{1}{2}+1\frac{3}{4})\div3$
14. $(3\frac{1}{2}\div2)+4\frac{3}{4}$
15. $2\frac{3}{4}\times(1\frac{1}{2}\div4)$
16. $3\frac{5}{8}+(1\frac{3}{4}\times2\frac{1}{2})-(1\frac{2}{3}\div5)$

6. Decimals

With the introduction of metrication and decimal currency the use of decimals has become commonplace, and is of much greater importance than the use of fractions. Decimals are usually much easier to use and less cumbersome than their fraction equivalents.

6.1 To convert a decimal to a fraction

A decimal can be written as a fraction with the denominator of 10, or a power of 10, depending on the number of places after the decimal point. This fraction can then be reduced to its lowest terms.

Example
(i) $3\cdot5 \quad = 3\frac{5}{10} \quad = 3\frac{1}{2}$
(ii) $4\cdot25 \quad = 4\frac{25}{100} = 4\frac{1}{4}$
(iii) $6\cdot125 = 6\frac{125}{1000} = 6\frac{1}{8}$
(iv) $0\cdot075 = \quad \frac{75}{1000} = \frac{3}{40}$

6.2 To convert a fraction to a decimal

A fraction can be converted to a decimal by dividing the numerator by the denominator.

Example
(i) $\frac{1}{2} = 1\div2 \quad = \dfrac{\cdot5}{2)1\cdot00}$

(ii) $\frac{3}{4} = 3\div4 \quad = \dfrac{\cdot75}{4)3\cdot00}$

(iii) $\frac{5}{16} = 5\div16 = \dfrac{\cdot3125}{16)5\cdot00}$

6.3   Addition and Subtraction

In adding and subtracting decimals the one important check is to make sure that the decimal points are under one another.

Example   (i) $2\cdot4 + 0\cdot35 + 11\cdot275$
                 $=$ $2\cdot4$
                          $0\cdot35$
                         $11\cdot275$

                         $\overline{14\cdot025}$

Example   (ii) $154\cdot93 - 13\cdot065$
                 $=$ $154\cdot930$
                           $13\cdot065$

                          $\overline{141\cdot865}$

6.4   Multiplication and Division by Powers of 10

One advantage of decimals is that multiplication and division by 10 or a power of 10 merely involves moving the decimal point; for multiplication it moves to the right, for division to the left.

Example $2\cdot46 \times 10\ \ \ = 24\cdot6$
                 $2\cdot46 \times 100\ = 246$
                 $2\cdot46 \times 1000 = 2460$
    Similarly $24\cdot6 \div 10\ \ \ = 2\cdot46$
                 $24\cdot6 \div 100\ = 0\cdot246$
                 $24\cdot6 \div 1000 = 0\cdot0246$

6.5   Multiplication

The rule for multiplying decimals is as follows:
   (i)   Multiply as if the two decimals were whole numbers.
  (ii)   Count the total number of decimal places in the two decimals being multiplied.
 (iii)   Place the decimal point to give the same total number of decimal places in the answer.
This rule can be shown in the following examples.

Examples   (i) $2 \cdot 4 \times 1 \cdot 2$ A total of 2 decimal places

$$= \frac{24}{10} \times \frac{12}{10}$$

$$= \frac{288}{100} = 2 \cdot 88 \quad \therefore \text{ 2 decimal places in answer}$$

Example   (ii) $2 \cdot 83 \times 1 \cdot 4$

$$= \left. \begin{array}{c} 2 \cdot 83 \\ 1 \cdot 4 \end{array} \right\} \text{ A total of 3 decimal places}$$

$$\begin{array}{r} 1132 \\ 2830 \\ \hline 3 \cdot 962 \end{array} \quad \therefore \text{ 3 decimal places in answer}$$

Example   (iii) $1 \cdot 74 \times 0 \cdot 027$

$$= \left. \begin{array}{c} 1 \cdot 74 \\ 0 \cdot 027 \end{array} \right\} \text{ A total of 5 decimal places}$$

$$\begin{array}{r} 1218 \\ 3480 \\ \hline 0 \cdot 04698 \end{array}$$
} In this case a 0 has to be placed after the decimal point to give 5 places of decimals in answer.

6.6   Division

In division of decimals we proceed as if dividing whole numbers, but before doing so we make the divisor a whole number.

As $6 \div 2 = 3$ Similary $2 \cdot 76 \div 1 \cdot 2$
and $60 \div 20 = 3$ and $27 \cdot 6 \div 12$ } will each have the same answer.

Example   (i) $2 \cdot 76 \div 1.2$ (2·76 and 1·2 are each multiplied by
$= 27 \cdot 6 \div 12$ 10 to make the divisor a whole
number)

$$= 12 \overline{)27 \cdot 6} \quad \begin{array}{r} 2 \cdot 3 \\ \end{array}$$

$$\begin{array}{r} 24 \\ \hline 36 \\ 36 \\ \hline \end{array}$$

Example (ii) $0.4775 \div 0.025$
               $= 477.5 \div \quad 25$ (Each multiplied by 1000)

$$
\begin{array}{r}
19.1 \\
25\overline{)477.5} \\
25 \\
\hline
227 \\
225 \\
\hline
25 \\
25 \\
\hline
\end{array}
$$

6.7   Decimal Places

Calculations involving decimals sometimes involve more places of decimals than is required for practical purposes. Also in division of decimals the answer may not terminate. In each of these cases it is necessary to round-off the answer to an appropriate number of decimal places. This is done by calculating to one more than the required number of places and, if the last figure is 5 or more, adding one to the last figure required.

Examples   (i) 1.333 $= 1.33$ to 2 d.p.
              (ii) 1.37 $= 1.4$ to 1 d.p.
              (iii) 4.8365 $= 4.837$ to 3 d.p.
              (iv) 5.698 $= 5.70$ to 2 d.p.
              (v) 6.997 $= 7.00$ to 2 d.p.

Exercise A.6

1. Express the following as fractions in their lowest terms:
    (i) 6.8 (ii) 3.64 (iii) 4.875 (iv) 0.0075 (v) 1.926
2. Express the following as decimals:
    (i) $\frac{1}{16}$ (ii) $\frac{7}{20}$ (iii) $\frac{5}{12}$ (iv) $\frac{9}{100}$ (v) $\frac{4}{15}$
3. Express the following to the number of decimal places indicated:
    (i) 2.467 (2 d.p.)   (iv) 4.594 (2 d.p.)
    (ii) 3.429 (1 d.p.)   (v) 7.3596 (3 d.p.)
    (iii) 0.0675 (3 d.p.)   (vi) 5.997 (2 d.p.)

4. $24 \cdot 06 + 0 \cdot 37 + 1 \cdot 523$
5. $3 \cdot 74 + 15 \cdot 62 + 0 \cdot 58$
6. $5 \cdot 68 - 2 \cdot 41$
7. $8 \cdot 09 - 3 \cdot 54$
8. $12 \cdot 24 + 1 \cdot 005 - 2 \cdot 93$
9. $4 \cdot 265 \times 100$
10. $0 \cdot 032 \times 1000$
11. $2 \cdot 45 \times 10000$
12. $5632 \div 100$
13. $16 \cdot 92 \div 100$
14. $1 \cdot 53 \div 1000$

15. $9 \cdot 24 \times 0 \cdot 8$
16. $15 \cdot 32 \times 1 \cdot 2$
17. $0 \cdot 015 \times 0 \cdot 007$
18. $24 \cdot 8 \div 0 \cdot 4$
19. $3 \cdot 72 \div 1 \cdot 2$
20. $(3 \cdot 74 + 0 \cdot 31) \div 0 \cdot 09$
21. $(5 \cdot 69 - 2 \cdot 21) \div 8 \cdot 7$
22. $\dfrac{0 \cdot 013 \times 1 \cdot 04}{1 \cdot 69 \ \times 0 \cdot 002}$
23. $\dfrac{0 \cdot 068 \times 13 \cdot 5}{0 \cdot 27 \ \times \ 1 \cdot 36}$

7. Test Paper A

1. £1·34 + £2·56 + £8·39
2. $(3749 \times 52) \div 18$
3. 464×25
4. $0 \cdot 43 \div 0 \cdot 026$ (to 1 d.p.)
5. $5 \cdot 27 \times 0.76$ (to 1 d.p.)
6. (£12·49 + £14·87) − £5·26
7. $0 \cdot 4 \times 0 \cdot 04$
8. $(3\frac{3}{4} + 4\frac{1}{6}) \times 1\frac{1}{8}$
9. $5\frac{1}{4} + (3\frac{1}{2} \times 1\frac{4}{7})$
10. $7\frac{7}{16} \div 1\frac{3}{4}$
11. $1756 \div 1000$
12. Write down in index form the prime factors of 2520
13. Find the LCM of 8, 12 and 15
14. Find the HCF of 16, 20 and 36
15. Express $\frac{3}{16}$ as a decimal
16. Write 0·72 as a fraction
17. Calculate the cost of 25 articles at £3·72 each
18. Calculate the cost of 1 article if 17 cost £5·27
19. A man earns £3·82 per hour. How much does this amount to for a week of 38 hours?
20. What is the total amount earned by 10 workmen if 5 earn £142·50 each, 3 earn £157·25 and 2 earn £170·40 each?

B. The metric and Imperial systems as currently used in business

1. The Metric and Imperial Systems

1.1 Metric Units

The Metric System of Weights and Measures has now been generally adopted throughout the world. Great Britain, which has retained its own system of Imperial weights and measures, is now committed to a change over to metric and gradually the use of Imperial units will be discontinued. The following table shows the prefixes common to all the metric system, together with a complete table of weight. Similar tables can be constructed for Length, Area and Volume, but only certain units are in common use. For instance, only grams and kilograms are in general use for measuring weight and, therefore, in the other tables only the commonly used units are shown.

Prefix	Multiple of basic unit	Weight	Length	Area	Volume
milli (m)	0·001	milligram (mg)	mm	mm²	
centi (c)	0·01	centigram (cg)	cm	cm²	cm³
deci (d)	0·1	decigram (dg)			dm³ (LITRE)
BASIC UNIT	1	GRAM (g)	METRE (m)	SQUARE METRE (m²)	CUBIC METRE (m³)
deca (da)	10	decagram (dag)			
hecto (h)	100	hectogram (hg)		hm² (HECTARE)	
kilo (k)	1000	kilogram (kg)	km	km²	

Note the units which have special names:
1. Hectare = 1 hm² = 10 000 m² (used for land measure).
2. Litre = 1 dm³ = 1000 cm³ (used for volumes of liquids).
3. Tonne = 1000 kg (used for weights of heavy loads).
The terms square hectometre and cubic decimetre are never used in practice.

1.2   Conversion of Units

It should be possible to convert units into the basic unit and vice-versa. It is unlikely, however, that conversion from a very small unit, say mm, to a much larger unit, the km, would ever be necessary, but all conversions can be made merely by moving a decimal point.

Examples (i) 2467 mm = 2·467 m (÷1000)
     (ii) 2·825 kg = 2825 g (×1000)
     (iii) 325 cm = 3250 mm (× 10)
     (iv) 485 m = 0·485 km (÷1000)

Take care when converting units of square measure and cubic measure, as illustrated below:

1 metre (m)   = 100 cm
1 square metre (m^2) = (100×100) cm^2 = 10 000 cm^2
1 cubic metre (m^3) = $(100 \times 100 \times 100)$ cm^3 = 1 000 000 cm^3

1.3   Imperial Units

Although the use of Imperial Units will gradually be discontinued, there are still some in common use and the complete replacement of Imperial Units by the metric system may take several years.
The following units are still in common use:

	Unit	*Conversions*	*Metric equivalents*
Weight	OUNCE	16 oz = 1 lb	1 kg = 2·2 lb
	POUND	2240 lb = 1 ton	
	TON		
Length	INCH	12 in = 1 ft	2·54 cm = 1 in
	FOOT	3 ft = 1 yd	1 m = 39·37 in
	YARD	1760 yd = 1 mile	
	MILE		8 km = 5 miles
Capacity	PINT	8 pt = 1 gallon	1 litre = 1·76 pint
	GALLON		

Exercise B1

1. Find the cost of 5·5 kg of apples at 92 p per kg.
2. Floor covering is priced at £2·25 per m². What is the cost of 18 m²?

3. Express the following in metres:
   (i) 2468 mm (ii) 127 cm (iii) 12 km
4. Calculate the cost of 500 g of sweets at £1·36 per kg.
5. What will 15 tonnes of hardcore cost if priced at £6·15 a tonne?
6. Calculate the cost of five 2½ litre tins of emulsion paint if priced at £2·54 per litre.
7. 5½ yds of cloth cost £6·82. What is the price per yd?
8. Calculate the cost of 18½ tons of coal at £37·24 a ton.
9. Calculate the cost of 12 gallons of petrol at 184·5 p per gallon.
10. A car travelled 420 km in 8 hours 30 minutes. Approximately how many km per hour does this amount to?

2. Decimal Currency

All the major currencies of the world are now decimal currencies with the basic unit divided into 100 parts. This means that a sum of money can be expressed as a decimal to two places and only the name of the basic unit need be used.

For instance, in the UK 1 pound 50 pence is written £1·50. Similarly in France 1 franc 50 centimes is written 1·50 francs and in the USA 1 dollar 50 cents is written $1·50.

The following are some of the major currencies in use:

Country	Currency		Rate of exchange (Jan. 1984)
USA	Dollar	= 100 cents	£1 = $1·45
Germany	Deutschmark	= 100 pfennige	£1 = 3·95 DM
France	Franc	= 100 centimes	£1 = 11·85 fr
Denmark	Krone	= 100 ore	£1 = 14·30 kr
Holland	Florin	= 100 cents	£1 = 4·44 fl

2.1 Rate of Exchange

The rate of exchange is the value of one currency in terms of another. The rates can fluctuate from day to day and current rates are published in the national press. The rates shown in the above table are those for January 1984.

Conversion of £s sterling into a foreign currency and vice-versa.

Example

    (i) To convert £20 into French francs if £1 = 11·85 francs.

$$£1 = 11·85 \text{ francs}$$
$$\therefore \quad £20 = 11·85 \times 20 \text{ francs}$$
$$= 237 \text{ francs}$$

Example

    (ii) To convert 200 US dollars into £s if £1 = 1·45 dollars.

$$1·45 \text{ dollars} = £1$$
$$1 \text{ dollar} = £\frac{1}{1·45}$$
$$200 \text{ dollars} = £\frac{1}{1·45} \times \frac{200}{1}$$
$$= £137·93$$

Exercise B2

1.　Your employer requires 200 French francs and 20 000 Italian lire. What will be the cost of this foreign currency at the following rates of exchange:

    £1 = 11·85 francs and £1 = 2360 lire?

2.　A person wishes to make a trip abroad and for incidental expenses decides to take francs to the value of £45 and pesetas to the value of £60. How many francs and pesetas will he obtain from his bank at the following rates of exchange:

    £1 = 11·82 francs and £1 = 222 pesetas.

3.　Apples in France are priced 6·35 francs per kg. Express this in pence per kg, given that £1 = 11·80 francs.

4.　A traveller has the opportunity of a visit to the USA by a charter flight costing £115 return. It is estimated that it will cost him a minimum of 45 dollars a day to live. Calculate in £s the minimum cost of this visit lasting 21 days if the rate of exchange is £1 = 1·51 dollars.

5.　A man takes a business trip to France, Switzerland and Italy. He changes travellers cheques as follows:

    £90 into French francs, £50 into Swiss francs,
        and £60 into Italian lire

On returning to England he has 95 French francs, 20 Swiss francs and 5200 Italian lire to change back into £ sterling. His English bank now offers the following rates of exchange:

£1 = 11·87 French francs.
£1 =   3·14 Swiss francs.
£1 = 2355 Italian lire.

Calculate, in English money, how much he spent on his trip abroad.

3. Calculations – the Area of a Rectangle

For most everyday purposes the calculation of the area of a rectangle is all that is required to deal with most problems on area. The unit of area is the square, e.g. the square millimetre, written mm^2, or the square metre (m^2) or square kilometre (km^2). It is, therefore, possible to measure an area by dividing it into a number of squares of the same size and counting the squares.

Example   Calculate the area of a rectangle 3 cm long by 2 cm wide.

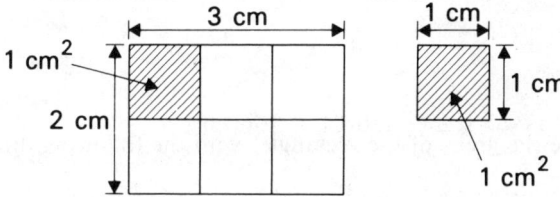

By counting the squares it can be seen that the area of the rectangle is 6 cm²

or   Area = length × breadth (l × b)
            = 3 cm × 2 cm
            = 6 cm²

Therefore for any rectangle:

$A = l \times b$ where l and b are in the same units.

or $l = \dfrac{A}{b}$

and $b = \dfrac{A}{l}$

It is important when using these formulae that the units are consistent.

Example   (i)   Calculate the area of piece of sheet metal 250 cm long by 40 cm broad.

$$\text{Area} = l \times b \qquad \text{where } l = 250 \text{ cm} = 2 \cdot 5 \text{ m}$$
$$= 250 \times 40 \qquad \qquad b = 40 \text{ cm} = 0 \cdot 4 \text{ m}$$
$$= 10\ 000 \text{ cm}^2$$

or $\text{Area} = 2 \cdot 5 \times 0 \cdot 4$
$$= 1 \text{ m}^2$$

Example   (ii)   Calculate the area of a piece of wood 11·4 cm long by 75 mm broad.

First write l and b in the same units.

$l = 11 \cdot 4$ cm	or $l = 114$ mm
$b = 7 \cdot 5$ cm	$b = 75$ mm
$A = 11 \cdot 4 \times 7 \cdot 5$	$A = 114 \times 75$
$= 85 \cdot 5$ cm²	$= 8550$ mm²

Exercise B3

1. Calculate the areas of the rectangles with the following dimensions:
    (i)   14 cm long and 8 cm broad.
    (ii)   2·5 m long and 10 cm broad.
    (iii) 1·62 m long and 1·24 m broad (answer in cm²).
    (iv)   15·65 km long and 13·20 km broad (answer to nearest km²).

2. Calculate the area of a pane of glass 1560 mm long by 650 mm wide.

3. A rectangle has an area of 17·5 m² and is 5 m long. Calculate its width.

4. Calculate the area of four walls of a room 4·8 m long by 3·9 m wide by 2·4 m high.

5. Calculate the floor area of a room which measutes 5·750 m long by 4·200 m wide.

6. A path 1 m wide is to be constructed around a garden plot which measures 16·5 m long and 8 m wide. Calculate the area of the path.

7. A rectangular field is 360 m long and 250 m wide. Calculate its area in hectares.

4. Test paper B

1. Express 2468 mm in metres.
2. Express 3·465 kg in grammes.
3. Express 72 560 m² in hectares.
4. Express 49 500 cm³ in litres.
5. Calculate the cost of 55 metres of cloth at £4·76 per metre.
6. Calculate the cost of 36 kg of apples at 58 p per kg.
7. If 65 kg of potatoes cost £9.75, what is the cost of 1 kg?
8. How many pesetas can I obtain for £16 if £1 = 223 pesetas?
9. How much will 374 francs be worth if £1 = 11·85 francs?
10. If petrol costs 184 p per gallon, how much is this per litre?
11. Calculate the area of a room 4·8 m long by 3·45 m wide.
12. Calculate the total wall area in a room 5·2 m long by 4·7 m wide and 2·5 m high (include areas of door and windows).
13. A rectangular field is 596 m long and 438 m wide. Calculate its area in hectares.
14. How many pieces of cloth 425 mm long can be cut from a roll of cloth 20 m long?
15. A car journey of 280 km took 6½ hours. How many km per hour does this represent?
16. Given that 1 kg = 2·2 lb convert 3756 lb to kg.
17. A holiday in France and Italy costs £175 plus 560 francs and 84 000 lire. Calculate the total cost in £s if £1 = 11·83 francs = 2360 lire.
18. What is the total weight in kg of 200 packets each weighing 125 g?
19. Express a speed limit of 30 mph in km/h.
20. Calculate the weight in tonnes of 20 m³ of material if 1 m³ weights 850 kg.

C. The purpose and use of approximations in business

1. Degrees of Accuracy

All measurement is approximate and its degree of accuracy depends on the measuring instruments and methods used. For instance, if we were to measure the width of a flat metal bar with an ordinary wooden rule we could probably measure it to the nearest millimetre. If, on the other hand, we used a micrometer, an engineer's measuring instrument, we could probably measure it to a hundredth part of a millimetre. We need different degrees of accuracy for different purposes. For all practical purposes it may only be necessary to measure the distance between two towns to the nearest kilometre, or the weight of a sack of potatoes to the nearest 500 grams.

2. Significant Figures

In measurement and in calculations based on this measurement we first have to decide the degree of accuracy required. If, for instance, it were possible to measure the distance between two places as 35·640 km, but an answer accurate to the nearest km was adequate, then this distance would be given as 36 km. This merely indicates that the actual distance lies somewhere between 35·5 km and 36·5 km. In this case we would say that the answer of 36 km was correct to two significant figures (2 s.f.).

Significant figures are those digits beginning with the first digit to the left which is not zero, and ending with the last digit which is not zero. There are certain exceptions where an end digit is significant.

Example   (i)   36 174 has 5 significant figures.
36 174 = 36 170 to 4 s.f.
36 174 = 36 200 to 3 s.f.
36 174 = 36 000 to 2 s.f.
36 174 = 40 000 to 1 s.f.

Example   (ii)   0·046 397 has 5 significant figures.
0·046 397 = 0·046 40 to 4 s.f.*
0·046 397 = 0·046   to 2 s.f.
0·046 397 = 0·05   to 1 s.f.

* This is an exception where the end zero is significant.

As with decimal places when correcting to a number of significant figures one more than the required number is calculated, and if this last figure is 5 or more 1 is added to the last significant figure.

3. Approximate answers

In all calculations, and especially when decimals are involved, you should make a rough approximation of the final answer as a check on your working. This can save many unnecessary errors from incorrect placing of the decimal point.

Example   (i) $24·6 \times 0·043$ to 3 s.f.

Approximate answer $25 \times 0·04$
$= 1·00$

Calculated answer $= 1·06$ to 3 s.f.

Example   (ii) $0·071 \div 0·0532$ to 3 s.f.

Approximate answer $= 0·07 \div 0·05$
$= 7 \div 5$
$= 1·4$

Calculated answer $= 1·33$ to 3 s.f.

Example   (iii)   £4336 ÷ 52 to 4 s.f.

$$\text{Approximate answer} = £4330 ÷ 50$$
$$= £86$$

$$\text{Calculated answer} = £83·38 \text{ to 4 s.f.}$$

Example   (iv) $£\dfrac{2576}{1} \times \dfrac{53}{365} \times \dfrac{15}{200}$

$$= £\dfrac{2576 \times 53 \times 3}{1 \times 73 \times 200}$$

$$\text{Approximate answer} = £\dfrac{2600 \times 150}{150 \times 100}$$

$$= £26$$

$$\text{Calculated answer} = £28·05$$

In each of these examples the calculated answer is sufficiently close to the approximate answer to feel reasonably certain that it is correct.

4.   How Many Significant Figures?

Having worked an approximate answer to a problem you can then readily determine how many significant figures are required in the calculated solution. For instance, in example (iv), which is a Simple Interest calculation, we see that 4 significant figures are required if the answer is to be to the nearest penny, but only two significant figures if the answer is required to the nearest £.

5.   Calculators

Small electronic calculators are now in common use, and by using them we avoid all the drudgery of long, tedious calculations. They provide almost instantaneous answers, and are extremely reliable. But at the same time mistakes can easily be made by pressing the wrong key or misplacing the decimal point. It is, therefore, desirable to check all work carried out on a calculator. If, for example, a calculator with a printout is being used for adding a number of items, then a visual check can be made that the correct items have been entered into the machine. If the calculator has no printout, then a double check of the calculation should be made. To safeguard against misplacing the decimal point it is advisable to determine an approximate answer first. This will then indicate whether the answer derived from the calculator is feasible.

6. Test Paper C

1. Correct the following to the degree of accuracy indicated:

(i)	2439 (3 s.f.)	(vi)	0·0699	(2 s.f.)
(ii)	47 905 (3 s.f.)	(vii)	12·0064	(3 s.f.)
(iii)	0·005 85 (1 s.f.)	(viii)	12·0064	(3 d.p.)
(iv)	49 587 (3 s.f.)	(ix)	15·739	(4 s.f.)
(v)	0·4515 (2 s.f.)	(x)	15·739	(2 d.p.)

2. For each of the following calculations determine an approximate answer. Then, by using a calculator, obtain an answer to the required degree of accuracy. Where a wide discrepancy occurs, re-check your work.

(i) $29·35 \times 2·11$ (2 d.p.)

(ii) $0·047 \times 15·94$ (2 s.f.)

(iii) $10·34 \times 18·36$ (5 s.f.)

(iv) $0·053 \times 0·039$ (4 d.p.)

(v) $0·053 \times 0·039$ (2 s.f.)

(vi) $759·4 \div 1·85$ (3 s.f.)

(vii) $0·007\ 82 \div 2·3$ (4 d.p.)

(viii) $1·937 \div 0·0031$ (1 d.p.)

(ix) $0·8449 \div 17$ (2 s.f.)

(x) $0·1 \div 9·32$ (2 d.p.)

(xi) $\dfrac{24·6 + (36·5 \times 15)}{4·36}$ (4 s.f.)

(xii) $\dfrac{3749 \times 27 \times 17·5}{1 \times 365 \times 100}$ (2 d.p.)

D. The nature and function of percentages

1. Percentages

1.1 Definition

A percentage is really a fraction with a denominator of 100, but in writing it down we use the symbol % and omit the denominator 100.

Example   (i) $7\% = \dfrac{7}{100}.$

(ii) $2\tfrac{1}{2}\% = \dfrac{2\tfrac{1}{2}}{100} = \dfrac{5}{200} = \dfrac{1}{40}.$

If we consider the fractions $\tfrac{15}{20}$ and $\tfrac{19}{25}$ we cannot tell at a glance which is the greater, but if we convert them to equivalent fractions with the same denominators we get

$$\text{(i)} \quad \frac{15}{20} = \frac{75}{100}$$

$$\text{and (ii)} \quad \frac{19}{25} = \frac{76}{100}$$

A comparison is now easy. Percentages are, therefore, used to compare quantities. Profit margins, price increases, rates of interest, are examples of quantities usually expressed and compared in terms of percentages.

1.2 To Convert a Fraction into a Percentage

Example   (i) $\tfrac{1}{2} = \tfrac{1}{2} \times \tfrac{100}{1}\% = 50\%$

(ii) $\tfrac{3}{4} = \tfrac{3}{4} \times \tfrac{100}{1}\% = 75\%$

(iii) $\tfrac{2}{5} = \tfrac{2}{5} \times \tfrac{100}{1}\% = 40\%$

A fraction is converted to a percentage by multiplying by 100.

1.3   To Convert a Decimal into a Percentage

Example   (i) $0.75 = 0.75 \times 100\% = 75\%$
              (ii) $0.4 \ = 0.4 \ \times 100\% = 40\%$
              (iii) $0.05 = 0.05 \times 100\% = \ 5\%$

A decimal is converted to a percentage by multiplying by 100.

1.4   To Convert a Percentage into a Fraction or Decimal

Example   (i) $40\% = \dfrac{40}{100} = \dfrac{2}{5}$

              or $40\% = \dfrac{40}{100} = 0.4$

Example   (ii) $12\tfrac{1}{2}\% = \dfrac{12\tfrac{1}{2}}{100} = \tfrac{1}{8}$

              or $12\tfrac{1}{2}\% = \dfrac{12.5}{100} = 0.125$

A percentage is converted to a fraction or decimal by dividing by 100.

1.5   To Calculate a Percentage of a Quantity

Example   (i) 15% of £25
                  $= £\dfrac{15}{100} \times \dfrac{25}{1} = £\dfrac{15}{4} = \underline{\underline{£3.75}}$

Example   (ii) $27\tfrac{1}{2}\%$ of £20
                  $= £\dfrac{27\tfrac{1}{2}}{100} \times \dfrac{20}{1} = £\dfrac{55}{200} \times \dfrac{20}{1}$

                  $= £\dfrac{55}{10} \qquad = \underline{\underline{£5.50}}$

1.6   To Calculate the 'Whole' Quantity from a Given Percentage

Example   (i)   If 8% of an amount $= £24$

              then 1% of the amount $= £\dfrac{24}{8}$

              and 100%
              (i.e. the whole amount) $= £\dfrac{24}{8} \times \dfrac{100}{1}$

                                  $= \underline{\underline{£300}}$

Example   (ii)   If 6%   = £90

then 1% $= £\dfrac{90}{6}$

and 100% (the whole) $= £\dfrac{90}{6} \times \dfrac{100}{1}$

$= £1500$

1.7   To Express One Quantity as a Percentage of Another

Example   (i)   If a student attends 36 classes out of a total of 40 classes his percentage attendance will be:

$$\frac{36}{40} \times \frac{100}{1}\% = 90\%$$

Example   (ii)   If a candidate in an examination obtains 42 marks out of a possible 60 marks his percentage mark will be:

$$\frac{42}{60} \times \frac{100}{1}\% = 70\%$$

1.8   Percentage Change—Increase and Decrease

Example   (i)   If the price of an article increases from £12·00 to £13·50 what will be the percentage increase?

New Price   = £13·50

Original Price   = £12·00

Increase   =   £1·50

Percentage increase $= \dfrac{1·50}{12·00} \times \dfrac{100}{1}\%$

$= \dfrac{150}{1200} \times \dfrac{100}{1}\% = 12·5\%$

Example   (ii)   If the number of employees in a factory decreases from 700 to 651 what percentage decrease does this represent?

Original number of
employees $= 700$
Present number $= 651$

Decrease $= 49$

Percentage decrease $= \frac{49}{700} \times \frac{100}{1} \% = \underline{7\%}$

Note: In examples (i) and (ii) the percentage increase and percentage decrease are calculated on the original quantities.

Example (iii) If the rent of a flat of £25 per week is increased by 20% what will the new rent be?

Method (i) £
Present rent $= 25$
Increase £$\frac{20}{100} \times \frac{25}{1} = 5$
New rent $= 30$

Method (ii)
If present rent $= 100$
then increase $= 20$

and new rent $= 120$

Ratio of present to
new rent $= 100:120$
∴ If present rent $= £25$

New rent $= £\frac{25}{1} \times \frac{120}{100} = £30$

Exercise D1

1. Express the following fractions as percentages:
   (i) $\frac{1}{5}$ (ii) $\frac{1}{4}$ (iii) $\frac{1}{3}$ (iv) $\frac{3}{16}$ (v) $1\frac{1}{8}$
2. Express the following decimals as percentages:
   (i) 0·5 (ii) 0·34 (iii) 0·175 (iv) 0·005 (v) 1·85
3. Express the following percentages as fractions in their lowest terms:
   (i) 15% (ii) $37\frac{1}{2}\%$ (iii) 140% (iv) $66\frac{2}{3}\%$ (v) 80%

4. Express the following percentages as decimals:
   (i) 40% (ii) $3\frac{3}{4}$% (iii) $27\frac{1}{2}$% (iv) 250% (v) 0·5%

5. Find the value of:
   (i)   24% of £15   (vi)   16% of 1825
   (ii) $7\frac{1}{2}$% of £8·40   (vii) $3\frac{1}{2}$% of 750 kg
   (iii) $1\frac{1}{4}$% of £1250   (viii) 2% of 4·25 litres
   (iv) $8\frac{1}{3}$% of £7·32   (ix)   15% of 4·200 metres
   (v)   2·5% of £3·90   (x) $\frac{1}{4}$% of 7256 000

6. Calculate the 'whole' quantity, given the following percentage values:
   (i)   15% = £10·80   (iii) 70% = £3·15
   (ii) $27\frac{1}{2}$% = £41·25 (iv)   9% = 31·5 kg

7. Express the first quantity as a percentage of the second:

   (i) $37\frac{1}{2}$p,   £1
   (ii) 340 g,   4·250 kg
   (iii) £3·75,   £14·50
   (iv) 239 mm,   4·500 m

8. A man who earns £142·75 per week receives a 10% increase. What will his new wage amount to?

9. An article is reduced in price from £12·50 to £11·30. What percentage decrease does this represent?

10. The population of a small town increased in one year from 12 250 to 13 170. What percentage increase does this represent?

2.   Profit and Loss

When an article is sold for more than it cost it is said to be sold at a profit, when sold for less it is said to be sold at a loss. The profit or loss can be expressed as a percentage of the cost price (C.P.) or as a percentage of the selling price (S.P.).

Example   (i) If a shopkeeper buys an article for £8 and sells it for £10, what percentage profit is made?

$$\text{S.P.} = 10\cdot00$$
$$\text{C.P.} = 8\cdot00$$
$$\text{Profit} = 2\cdot00$$

$$\text{Percentage Profit} = \frac{2}{8} \times \frac{100}{1}\% = 25\%$$
(based on C.P.)

$$\text{Percentage Profit} = \frac{2}{10} \times \frac{100}{1}\% = 20\%$$
(based on S.P.)

Example (ii)   An article is bought for £15 and sold at a profit of 30% on C.P. What is the S.P.?

Method (i)   C.P.   = £15·00

$$\text{Profit} = £\frac{30}{100} \times \frac{15}{1} = £\ 4\cdot50$$

S.P.   = £19·50

Method (ii)   If C.P. = 100
Profit = 30

S.P.   = 130

Ratio C.P.:S.P. = 100:130
∴   If C.P. = £15

$$\text{S.P.} = £\frac{15}{1} \times \frac{130}{100} = £19\cdot50$$

Example (iii)   An article is bought for 40p and sold at a loss of 15% of C.P. What is the S.P.?

If C.P.   = 100
Loss   = 15 (15% of C.P.)

S.P.   = 85

Ratio C.P.:S.P. = 100:85
∴   If C.P. = 40 p

$$\text{Then S.P.} = \frac{40}{1} \times \frac{85}{100} = 34p$$

Example (iv)   An article costing £40 is sold at a profit of 20% of S.P. What is the S.P.?

$$\begin{array}{ll}
\text{If S.P.} & = 100 \\
\text{Profit} & = \underline{20} \quad (20\% \text{ of S.P.}) \\
\text{and C.P.} & = \underline{80} \\
\text{Ratio C.P.:S.P.} & = 80:100 \\
\therefore \text{ If C.P.} & = £40 \\
\text{Then S.P.} & = £\dfrac{40}{1} \times \dfrac{100}{80} = £50
\end{array}$$

Example   (v)   An article costs £22 and is sold at a loss of 10% of S.P. What is the S.P.?

$$\begin{array}{ll}
\text{If S.P.} & = 100 \\
\text{Loss} & = \underline{10} \quad (10\% \text{ of S.P.}) \\
\text{and C.P.} & = \overline{110} \quad (\text{Note C.P. is greater than} \\
& \text{S.P.}) \\
\text{Ratio C.P.:S.P.} & = 110:100 \\
\therefore \text{ S.P.} & = £\dfrac{22}{1} \times \dfrac{100}{110} = £20
\end{array}$$

Note 1.   In this example C.P. is greater than S.P. Therefore, C.P. has to be multiplied by a factor less than 1, i.e. $\frac{100}{110}$, to arrive at S.P.

2.   In all these examples a simple check on your answer can be made as follows:

$$\begin{array}{ll}
\text{Check on example (v)} & £ \\
\text{Given C.P.} & = 22 \\
\text{Calculated S.P.} & = 20 \\
\therefore \text{ Loss} & = \underline{2} \\
\text{\% Loss} & = \dfrac{2}{20} \times \dfrac{100}{1} \% = 10\% \\
\text{(based on S.P.)} &
\end{array}$$

Exercise D2

1.   Calculate the missing figures in the following table. The profit or loss is to be calculated as a percentage of the *Cost Price*.

	C.P.	Profit/Loss	S.P.
(i)	£3	Profit 20%	—
(ii)	£4·75	Profit 16%	—
(iii)	75p	Loss 14%	—
(iv)	—	Profit 15%	£16·10
(v)	—	Loss 6¼%	£1·95
(vi)	£12	—	£13·50
(vii)	£17·50	—	£15·00

2. Calculate the missing figures in the following table. The profit or loss is to be calculated as a percentage of the *Selling Price*.

	C.P.	Profit/Loss	S.P.
(i)	30p	Profit 25%	—
(ii)	—	Profit 16%	£15·25
(iii)	£5·52	Loss 15%	—
(iv)	—	Loss 7½%	£7·60
(v)	£21·70	Profit 22½%	—
(vi)	£16·17	—	£19·60
(vii)	£5·89	—	£4·75

3. Simple Interest

3.1 Simple Interest Formula

Interest is the charge made when a sum of money is borrowed for a period of time. The interest is known as Simple Interest when it is calculated on the original sum borrowed, and hence remains the same for each year. The sum borrowed is known as the Principal and the Principal plus the accrued interest is known as the Amount. The interest charged is calculated as a percentage of the Principal for each year of the loan.

Example   (i) If £200 is borrowed at 5% per annum for 3 years, how much interest will have to be paid?
Interest on £100 at 5% for 1 year = £5
Interest on £200 at 5% for 1 year = £10
Interest on £200 at 5% for 3 years = £30

This calculation can be obtained by using the formula

$$I = P \times \frac{R}{100} \times N$$

Where I = Interest
P = Principal
R = Rate per cent
N = No. of years

In example (i)
P = £200
R = 5%
N = 3 years

and I = $£\frac{200 \times 5 \times 3}{100}$ = £30

When the loan is for part of a year N is calculated as a number of days and then expressed as a fraction of a year, e.g. $N = \frac{\text{No. of days.}}{365}$

Example (ii) If £600 is borrowed on 4th March at 8% p.a. and repaid on 16th May, how much interest will be paid? No. of days = 27 in March
30 in April
16 in May

Total 73

Note: We do not count both 4th March and 16th May. Only one of these dates is counted for interest purposes, in this example just 16th May.

P = £600
R = 8%
$$N = \frac{73}{365}$$

and I = $£\frac{600}{1} \times \frac{8}{100} \times \frac{73}{365}$

= $\frac{48}{5}$ = £9·60

3.2 Inverse Problems

The Simple Interest formula involves fourth quantities I, P, R and N. Given any three of these, the four can be calculated. The formula then has to be re-arranged as follows:

(i) $\quad P = \dfrac{100 \times I}{R \times N}$ $\qquad$ (ii) $\quad R = \dfrac{100 \times I}{P \times N}$ $\qquad$ (iii) $\quad N = \dfrac{100 \times I}{P \times R}$

Notice the similarity between these formulae which will help you to remember them.

Example (i) If $\quad$ P = £250
$$I = £70$$
$$N = 4 \text{ years}$$
$$\text{Then } R = \frac{100 \times I}{P \times N} = \frac{100 \times 70}{250 \times 4} = \underline{\underline{7\%}}$$

Example (ii) If $\quad$ P = £1000
$$I = £240$$
$$R = 8\%$$
$$\text{Then } N = \frac{100 \times I}{P \times R} = \frac{100 \times 240}{1000 \times 8} = \underline{\underline{3 \text{ years}}}$$

Exercise D3

1. Calculate the missing items in the following examples:

	Principal	Interest	Amount	Rate % p.a.	Time
(i)	£1000	—	—	5	3 yrs.
(ii)	£120	—	—	5	100 days
(iii)	£2000	£420	—	$3\frac{1}{2}$	—
(iv)	£1836	—	£1854·36	$1\frac{1}{4}$	—
(v)	£7300	£204·40	—	—	292 days
(vi)	—	£249·48	—	$8\frac{1}{4}$	4 yrs.

2. A man borrowed £6000 from his bank on 22nd May at 8% per annum. If the loan was repaid on 3rd August the same year how much interest was payable?

3. A man borrowed £1460 from his bank for a period of 20 days and was charged £16 interest. What was the rate of interest charged?

4. A man borrowed 32 120 francs for 45 days at $7\frac{1}{2}$%. How much interest did he pay?

5. £400 was borrowed on 27th September and repaid with interest at 15% p.a. on 30th November the same year. Calculate to the nearest penny the amount repaid.

4. Compound Interest and Depreciation

4.1 Compound Interest

When money is invested at Compound Interest the interest due is added to the capital invested at agreed intervals of time. In this way the Principal, i.e. the sum on which interest is calculated, increases from one period to the next. With Simple Interest it is assumed that the interest is actually paid out and, therefore, the Principal remains constant. The value of the investment at any time is known as the Amount.

Example   (i) Calculate the Compound Interest on £500 invested at 10% per annum for 3 years.

	£
Principal 1st year	= 500·00
Interest 1st year	= 50·00
Principal 2nd year	= 550·00
Interest 2nd year	= 55·00
Principal 3rd year	= 605·00
Interest 3rd year	= 60·50
Amount at end of 3rd year	= 665·50

Compound Interest = Amount−Original Principal
              = £665·50 −£500
              = £165·50

Example (ii) Using the same figures as in example (i), but calculating Simple Interest, we get

$$\text{Simple Interest} = \pounds\frac{500}{1} \times \frac{10}{100} \times \frac{3}{1}$$
$$= \pounds150$$

Many forms of investment and loans are based on Compound Interest. One is the National Savings Bank, where interest at 5% is added to the balance on the account at the end of each year.

Example (iii) If £400 is placed in a National Savings Account paying 3% per annum Compound Interest, how much will be in the account after two complete years, assuming no withdrawals?

	£
Principal 1st year	= 400
Interest 1st year	= 12
Principal 2nd year	= 412
Interest 2nd year	= 12·36
Amount after 2 years	= 424·36

Note: To find 3% of £412   1% = £4·12
                           3% = £4·12 × 3
                              = £12·36

4.2 Compound Interest Tables

The method used in examples (i) and (iii) shows how compound interest can be calculated, but this would be a totally unsuitable method for business use. Therefore, tables, which give the Amount of £1 invested at various rates of interest are used. The following is an extract from a set of tables giving values correct to 5 places of decimals:

Years	2½%	3%	3½%	4%	4½%	5%
1	1·025 00	1·030 00	1·035 00	1·040 00	1·045 00	1·050 00
2	1·050 63	1·060 90	1·071 23	1·081 60	1·092 03	1·102 50
3	1·076 89	1·092 73	1·108 72	1·124 86	1·141 17	1·157 63
4	1·103 81	1·125 51	1·147 52	1·169 86	1·192 52	1·215 51
5	1·131 41	1·159 27	1·187 69	1·216 65	1·246 18	1·276 28
.	.	.	.	.	.	.
.	.	.	.	.	.	.
.	.	.	.	.	.	.
10	1·280 09	1·343 92	1·410 60	1·480 24	1·552 97	1·628 89
.	.	.	.	.	.	.
.	.	.	.	.	.	.
.	.	.	.	.	.	.
20	1·638 62	1·806 19	1·989 79	2·191 23	2·411 71	2·653 30

From these tables it will be seen that:

the Amount of £1 at 2½% for 1 year   = £1·025 00
the Amount of £1 at 2½% for 20 years   = £1·638 62
and the Amount of £1000 at 2½% for 20 years = £1·638 62 × 1000
                                            = £1638·62

4.3 Depreciation

A business may own machinery, equipment and other property, known as its assets. These assets will depreciate in value all the time, and each year the depreciation has to be estimated and charged as a business expense. Money also has to be set aside to pay for replacements when necessary. There are a number of ways of calculating depreciation – one of these is the reducing balance method whereby the depreciation is calculated as a percentage of the book value of the equipment at the beginning of the year.

Example   A business buys machinery costing £10 000. It decides to calculate the depreciation each year at 20% of its value at the beginning of the year. Calculate the book value after 3 complete years.

	£
Cost of machinery	= 10 000
Depreciation 1st year	= 2 000
Book value beginning 2nd year =	8 000
Depreciation 2nd year	= 1 600
Book value beginning 3rd year =	6 400
Depreciation 3rd year	= 1 280
Book value at end 3rd year	= 5 120

Exercise D4

1. Find, to the nearest £1, the Compound Interest (payable yearly) on the following:

      (i)   £500 at 6% for 3 years.
      (ii) £750 at 8% for 3 years.
      (iii) £2500 at $6\frac{3}{4}$% for 4 years.
      (iv) £1250 at 4% for 5 years.

2. How much will £250 amount to after 5 complete years if invested at $9\frac{1}{2}$% per annum compound interest?
3. The value of a machine depreciates each year by 10% of its value at the beginning of the year. Its value when new is £1250. Find its value after 6 complete years.
4. Using Compound Interest tables, find to the nearest £1, how much the investments will amount to after the periods stated:

      (i)   £500 at 4% p.a. for 3 years.
      (ii) £750 at $4\frac{1}{2}$% p.a. for 20 years.
      (iii) £2500 at 3% p.a. for 10 years.
      (iv) £1250 at $2\frac{1}{2}$% p.a. for 4 years.

5. A business borrowed £40 000 at 15% p.a. Compound Interest, the interest payable yearly, and repaid £7500 at the end of each year. How much was still owing at the end of the 3rd year?

5.   Test Paper D

1. Express as percentage (i) $\frac{5}{8}$ (ii) 0·045.
2. Express as decimals   (i) 27%   (ii) 72·5%.
3. Calculate 17·5% of £24·80.
4. Express £3·50 as a percentage of £10·50.
5. The price of an article increases from £1·25 to £1·55. What percentage increase does this represent?
6. An article priced at £3·20 is marked down in price by 15%. What is its selling price?
7. An article bought for £2·20 is sold at a profit of 15% of cost price. What is its selling price?
8. An article bought for £2·20 is sold at a profit of 15% of selling price. What is its selling price?
9. Calculate the simple interest on £350 at 8·5% for 5 years.
10. Calculate, to the nearest penny, the simple interest on £1000 at $9\frac{1}{2}$% p.a. for the period from 24th March to 14th August of the same year.
11. The sum of £120 invested for 2 years earns £18·60 interest. What rate of simple interest does this represent?
12. What sum of money invested at 8·25% simple interest will earn £547·80 interest over 4 years?
13. Calculate, to the nearest £, the compound interest on £500 at 6·5% p.a. for 4 years. Interest is added yearly.
14. Calculate the book value, after 3 complete years, of a machine purchased for £1500 which is depreciated at the rate of 12·5% p.a. of its value at the beginning of each year. (Give answer to nearest £10.)
15. Using a set of Compound Interest tables calculate how much £2500 will amount to if invested at $4\frac{1}{2}$% p.a. for 20 years.

E. The use of the average in business

1. The Arithmetic Mean

In its most commonly used form the word 'average' refers to the arithmetic mean of a number of quantities. This is obtained by dividing the sum of the quantities by the number of quantities.

Example (i) If the monthly takings in a small business for a six-monthly period were: £865, £920, £879, £912, £940, £932, what were the average monthly takings?

Total takings $= £(865+920+879+912+940+932)$

$= £5448$

No. of months $= 6$

Average takings per month (or Arithmetic mean) $= £\dfrac{5448}{6} = £908$

Example (ii) The takings of a shop for one year (52 weeks) were £28 486. What were the average takings each week calculated to the nearest £?

Takings for year $= £28\ 486$

Average weekly takings (or Arithmetic mean) $= \dfrac{£28\ 486}{52}$

$= £548$ (to nearest £)

2. The 'Weighted' Average

In any set of data some quantities may be repeated. If this is so, due 'weighting' must be given to those items to arrive at a true average.

Example   The owner of an apple orchard graded his crop in
two classes and packed them in boxes containing
10 kg each. He sold 20 boxes at £1·90 per box and
30 boxes at £1·40 per box. What average price per
kg did he receive for his apples?

                                                                        £

S.P. of 20 boxes (200 kg) @ £1·90 each = 38·00
S.P. of 30 boxes (300 kg) @ £1·40 each = 42·00

∴   S.P. of 500 kg   = 80·00

Average price per kg $= \dfrac{8000}{500}p$

                                          $= 16p$

Note: In this example due 'weighting' is given to the larger number of
cheaper apples sold.

3.   The Median

The Median is the middle item in a series of quantities that have been
arranged in order.

Example   (i)   The weekly sales in a department store for five consecutive weeks were as follows: £2137, £2140,
£2139, £1084, £2135. Identify the Median.
Arranged in order of value we get:

£1084   £2135   │ £2137 │   £2139   £2140

∴   The Median = £2137

Example   (ii)   Identify the Median of the following quantities
arranged in order:

28   36   │ 48   50 │   54   57

In this case there is no middle item, therefore the
Median must lie between 48 and 50. The simple

solution in this case is to take the arithmetic mean of the two middle items.

$$\therefore \quad \text{The Median} = \frac{48+50}{2} = 49$$

4. The Mode

The Mode is a value or group of values which occurs most frequently in a set of data.

Example The following are the units of daily output for a factory for 10 working days. Identify the Mode output.

Day	1	2	3	4	5	6	7	8	9	10
Output	79	80	83	78	80	80	81	82	75	79

We see that 80 occurs most frequently.

$$\therefore \quad \text{The 'Mode' output} = 80 \text{ units}$$

5. The Uses of the Arithmetic Mean, Median and Mode

These are the three forms of average that are the most commonly used in statistical calculations. We have to decide which is the best one to use for any given situation.

The Arithmetic Mean is widely used because it can be calculated accurately, but it must be remembered that 'averaging' a small number of quantities only does not give a very reliable result. An unreliable result may also occur if there is an 'exceptional' value contained in the set of data.

The use of the Median minimises the effect of an exceptional item, as the following example shows:

Example The rainfall, in mm, in a town for the month of August in seven consecutive years was as follows:

33   38   29   35   10   39   39

Arranging these in order we get:

$$10 \qquad 29 \qquad 31 \qquad \boxed{33} \qquad 35 \qquad 38 \qquad 39$$

(i) The Median value = 33 mm

(ii) The arithmetic mean of these values $= \dfrac{10+29+31+33+35+38+39}{7}$

$$= \frac{215}{7} = 30\cdot7 \text{ mm}$$

(iii) The arithmetic mean excluding the 'exceptional' value of 10 mm $= \dfrac{29+31+33+35+38+39}{6}$

$$= \frac{205}{6} = 34 \text{ mm}$$

In this case it can be seen that the Median is probably a more useful statistic than the Arithmetic Mean of all the values.

The Mode has many uses in business. It indicates the most typical value. For a manufacturer it would indicate which article to produce in the largest quantity as 'Mode' size is the most popular size, and therefore, the one for which there is likely to be the greatest demand.

6. Test Paper E

1. Calculate the Arithmetic Mean of the following:
    £245   £372   £843   £527   £948

2. Calculate the average wage per worker if 8 earn £176·50 per week, 7 earn £182·40 per week and 5 earn £183·60 per week.

3. Identify the 'Median' in each of the following sets of data:

    (i)   £24   £36   £19   £43   £28   £29   £31
    (ii) 84   76   39   47   81   56   73   62
    (iii) 61·8   63·2   64·5   61·2   64·1   85·9   65·9   62·3   63·6

4. Identify the 'Mode' in the following set of data:

    30   45   50   30   60   70   45   25   55   15   45   50

5. The sales of men's shoes of different sizes are given in the table:

Size	$7\frac{1}{2}$	8	$8\frac{1}{2}$	9	$9\frac{1}{2}$	10	$10\frac{1}{2}$	11
No. sold	15	50	84	85	52	23	12	8

What is the 'Mode' size?

6. A tradesman's weekly takings in one month were as follows:

£252·65   £248·37   £251·49   and   £245·39

  (i) What were the weekly average takings?

 (ii) What might he expect to take in one year (52 weeks) estimated from this average?

7. In the first five months of the year the sales in a small department of a store were valued at £2239, £1846, £1879, £2124 and £2259. What must the June sales amount to in order to achieve a monthly average of £2200?

8. A train leaves Kings Cross station and travels 280 km to its destination in 2 hrs 40 mins. If the return journey to Kings Cross takes 2 hrs 30 mins calculate by how much the average speed has increased.

9. The following are the units of daily output of a factory for 12 working days.

Day	1	2	3	4	5	6	7	8	9	10	11	12
Output	80	82	79	80	86	78	66	24	46	58	66	72

Find (i) the average daily output

      (ii) the Median output

Which is the more reliable estimate of the factory's output?

10. In a small business the following annual salaries are paid: 1@£18 500, 1@£10 000, 1@£9250, 1@£8950 and 6@£7500.

Find (i) the Median salary.

     (ii) the Arithmetic Mean salary.

     (iii) the Arithmetic Mean salary excluding the one exeptionally high salary.

11. In a food store the number of packets of frozen peas sold on each of 15 days was as follows:

Day	1	2	3	4	5	6	7	8	9	10	11	12	13	14	15
No. packets	7	55	96	38	17	55	5	49	28	83	72	66	23	41	14

Find   (i) the Median.
   (ii) the Mode.
   (iii) the Arithmetic Mean number of packets sold daily, giving the answer to the nearest whole number.
   (iv) the number of extra packets needed to be sold on day 15 to make the Arithmetic Mean up to 45.

12. In a small business the average gross profit is 25% of total sales. The expenses of running the business are £15 200, and in addition the owner wishes to derive an annual income of £16 000 from the business. What will the average weekly sales need to be to achieve this income?

F. The use of visual presentation of business data

Business data is frequently presented in the form of charts or diagrams. Statistical information presented in this way can usually be more readily understood than when presented in tabular form. Various types of presentation can be used.

1. Bar Charts

A bar chart represents a variable quantity by drawing bars proportional in length to the variable. A suitable scale must be chosen and this should start from zero to avoid giving a false impression.

Example In a small business the units of production for the first six months of a year were as follows:

Month	Jan	Feb	Mar	April	May	June
Output	2400	2350	2800	2000	3050	3250

Represent this information as a bar chart.

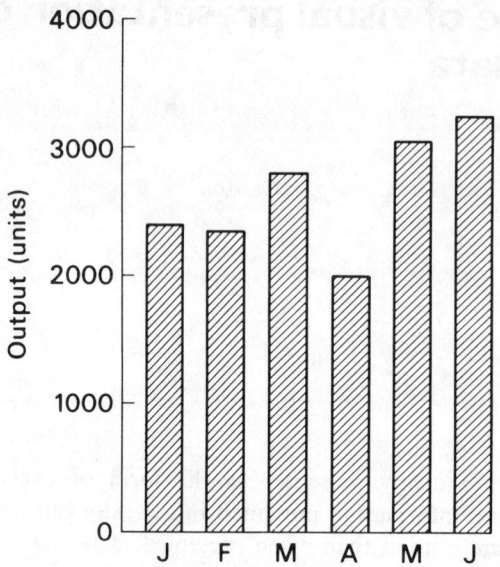

In this example the chart could not be used to read off very accurately the actual output, but it does show, at a glance, the general upward trend in output over the six-month period.

2. Component Bar Charts

A component bar chart will show the way a variable quantity is divided among its components.

Example   The sales of a company over a four-year period divided into 'home-market' sales and 'export' sales were as follows:

	1980		1981		1982		1983	
Home-market (£)	50 000	67%	55 000	65%	51 000	63%	56 000	59%
Export (£)	25 000	33%	29 000	35%	30 000	37%	39 000	41%
Total (£)	75 000	100%	84 000	100%	81 000	100%	95 000	100%

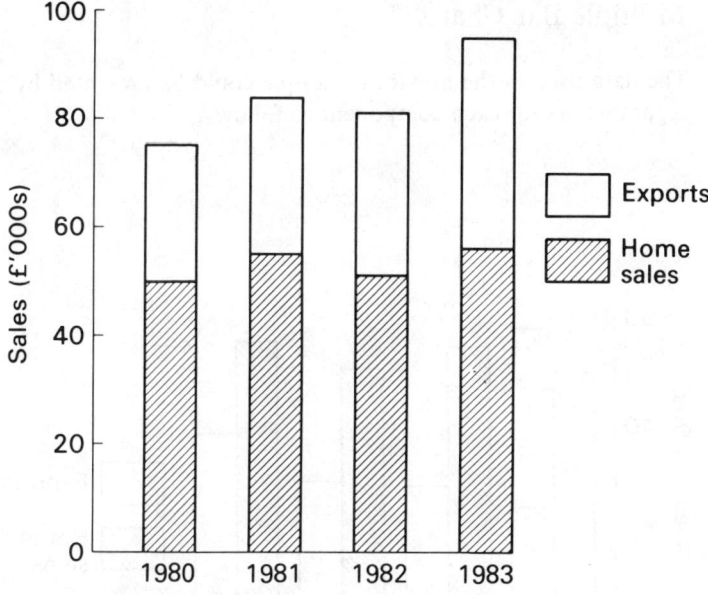

Although the reading of actual sales figures from this chart is not easy this form of presentation indicates quite clearly the changing ratio of exports to home-sales over the four-year period.

3.   Multiple Bar Charts

The data used in the previous example could be presented by using separate bars for each component as follows:

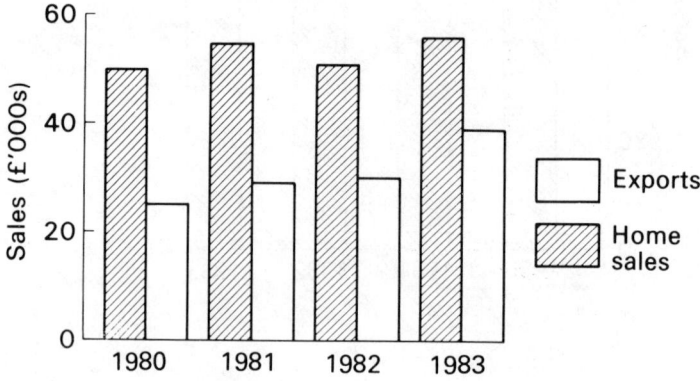

This form of presentation makes the comparison of the components easy although 'total' sales figures for each year can only be obtained by adding the figures for the individual components.

4.   Percentage Component Bar Charts

A percentage component bar chart is used when it is required to represent the components as percentages of the whole. Each bar will be the same length to represent 100%. The example given in section 2 includes the percentages and these can be represented as follows:

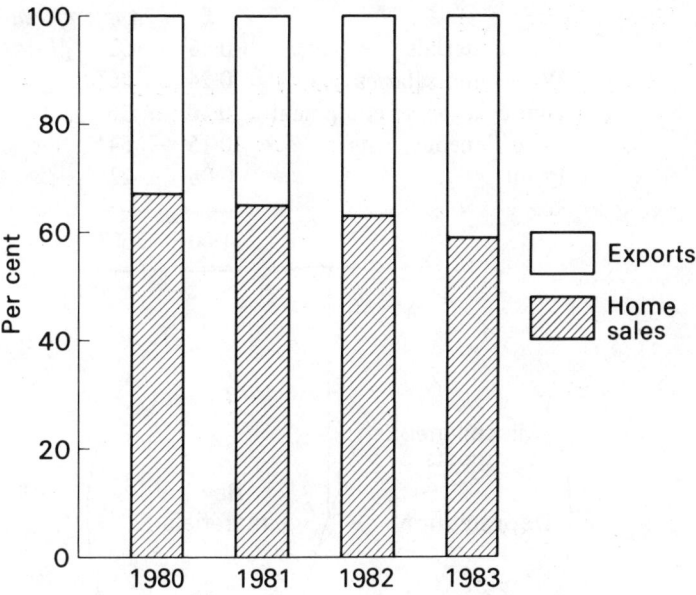

This chart shows quite clearly the increasing proportion of the total sales which are exports.

5. Pie Charts

The pie chart is used to represent the relative sizes of a number of quantities. It can, therefore, be used as an alternative to the component bar chart. A pie chart is a circle divided into a number of segments, the angle of each segment being proportional to the quantity represented.

Example A businessman estimates that each £1 received from the sale of his products is used as follows:

	£	*Angle at centre*
Raw materials	0·45	162° $(\frac{45}{100} \times \frac{360}{1})$
Wages and salaries	0·24	86°
Depreciation of equipment	0·10	36°
Miscellaneous costs	0·15	54°
Profit	0·06	22°
	1·00	360°

6. Graphs

When a large number of items of data are involved a graph may be a better form of presentation than a bar chart or pie chart. The data is plotted as a series of points, and the points then joined. The vertical axis is used for the variable quantity and the horizontal axis for the non-variable quantity.

Example   The number of young people registered as unemployed in each month of a one-year period was as follows:

Month	Ju	Jy	A	S	O	N
Unemployed (000's)	50	90	192	150	105	80
Month	D	J	F	M	A	M
Unemployed (000's)	70	80	68	58	57	70

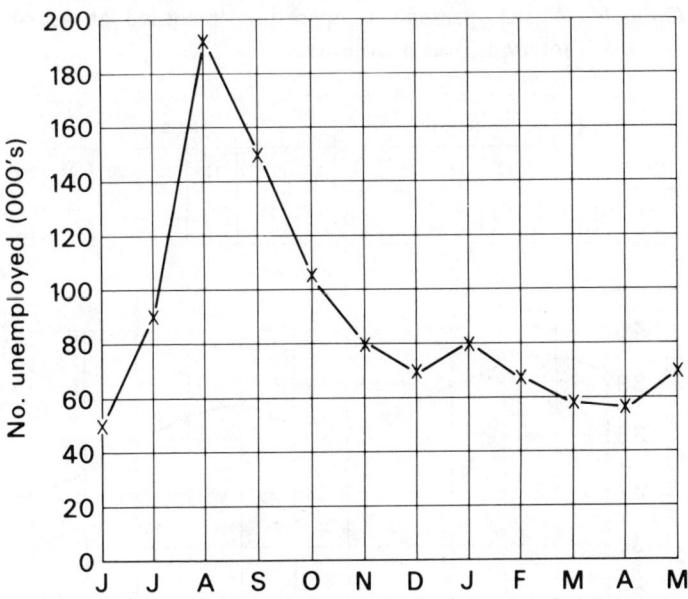

This graph plots the statistics from June of one year to May the following year. It shows clearly the trend in the figures from the time young people start leaving school at the end of the summer term to the peak unemployment in August and the gradual drop as jobs are found. An expected increase in unemployment takes place in January when further school leavers enter the employment market.

7.   Locus Graphs

When the graph has to represent a continuously changing set of data such as room or body temperature the graph will be drawn as a smooth curve linking together the points that have been recorded and plotted.

Example   A sick person's temperature, recorded at four-hourly intervals, was as follows:

	Nov. 1					Nov. 2						Nov. 3	
Time h	8	12	16	20	24	4	8	12	16	20	24	4	8
Temp. °C	39·2	39·5	39·3	39·0	38·5	38·3	38·3	38·6	38·4	37·9	37·4	37·0	36·9

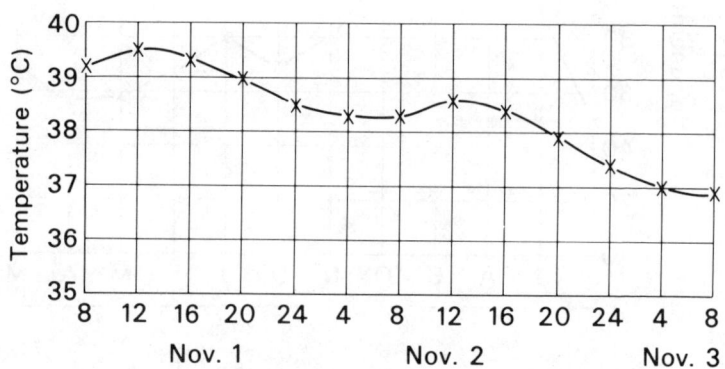

The smooth curve used in a graph of this sort gives a truer picture of what actually happens than would be given if the points plotted were joined by a series of straight lines. Furthermore, a limited range of about 35° to 40° is all that is necessary for the vertical scale. To start this scale at 0°C would be unrealistic.

8. Test Paper F

1. The number, in thousands, of young persons entering the labour market in the years 1977–81 was as follows:

1977	1978	1979	1980	1981
671	689	703	718	725

    Represent this information as a bar chart.

2. The table below gives the share in percentage terms of the principal sources of energy used in the UK in recent years. Illustrate this information as a percentage component bar chart.

Fuel	1978	1979	1980	1981
Petroleum	41·7	39·9	37·9	35·7
Coal	34·6	35·6	35·9	36·8
Natural gas and others	23·7	24·5	26·2	27·5
	100·0	100·0	100·0	100·0

3. The numbers of men and women employed in a small factory on the same day in four consecutive years are as follows:

	1980	1981	1982	1983
Men	64	66	59	57
Women	36	41	50	62
Total	100	107	109	119

Illustrate this information as (i) a component bar chart and (ii) a multiple bar chart.

4. Sums of money advanced by Building Societies, Local Authorities, Insurance Companies and Banks for house purchase in the two years 1971 and 1981 were as follows:

	Sum advanced (£ million)	
	1971	1981
Building Societies	1600	6330
Local Authorities	110	250
Insurance Companies	70	240
Banks	90	2240
	1870	9060

Draw a pie chart to illustrate this information for each of these years.

5. The break-down of personal income and expenditure in percentage terms for the year 1981 was as follows:

Income from:	%	Expenditure on:	%
Employment	63	Consumption	66
Self-employment	7	National Insurance and other contributions	6
Rents, dividends and interest	17	Taxes	15
Social security	13	Savings, etc.	13
	100		100

Draw pie charts to illustrate this information.

6. The consumer price indices for a number of countries in recent years are listed below:

	1978	1979	1980	1981
United Kingdom	100	113	134	150
France	100	111	126	143
Germany	100	104	110	116
Japan	100	104	112	117
USA	100	111	126	140

Illustrate this information in a suitable chart.

7. The temperatures, in °C, recorded in a room at given times were as follows:

Time	9.00	10.00	11.00	12.00	13.00	14.00	15.00	16.00
Temp.	16	16·5	17·8	18·8	18·7	19·2	18·0	17·5

Draw a graph to show the variations in room temperature and from your graph state:
   (i) the probable room temperature at 13.30 hours
and (ii) the times when the probable temperature was 18·2°C.

8. The number of children born annually in recent years in the United Kingdom is shown below:

Year	1972	1973	1974	1975	1976	1977	1978	1979	1980	1981
No. of births (thousands)	834	700	737	698	676	657	687	735	754	731

Plot this data on a suitable graph.

Part II

G. Cash and bank accounts

1. The Cash Book

The most fundamental record that has to be kept in business is the record of money received and payments made. Some of these transactions will be in cash, others by cheque. The small shopkeeper, for instance, will receive cash for most of his sales, and then pay the cash into the bank. But most of his payments for purchasing goods, etc. will be made by cheque. Most people these days will have a bank account, and in many cases they will be paid by cheque or have their salaries credited direct to their bank account. Periodically they will receive a statement from the bank showing transactions made on the account. For the businessman it is essential, and for the individual desirable, to keep his own record of these transactions, and then to verify that the bank's record as shown on the bank statement is correct.

The following shows how transactions could be recorded in a simple cash book. The receipts or deposits in the bank are shown on the left, and the payments or withdrawals from the bank shown on the right.

Cash Book					
Date	*Receipts*	*Amount*	*Date*	*Payments*	*Amount*
Jan. 1	Balance	254·50	Jan. 4	Cash	20·00
„ 28	Salary	324·36	„ 11	Rent	65·00
			„ 11	Cash	50·00
			„ 16	Electricity bill	19·28
			„ 18	Cash	40·00
			„ 28	Car repairs	24·30
			„ 31	Balance	360·28
		578·86			578·86
Feb. 1	Balance	360·28			

2. The Bank Statement

A statement from the bank for the same period might show these transactions in the following manner:

Bank Statement – The National Bank Ltd.				
Date	*Detail*	*Debits*	*Credits*	*Balance*
Jan. 1	Balance forward:			254·50
6	920 123	20·00		234·50
13	920 124	65·00		
13	920 125	50·00		119·50
18	920 126	19·28		100·22
19	920 127	40·00		
30	920 128	24·30		35·92
31	Cheque		324·36	360·28

Note
   (i)   The numbers shown in the 'Detail' column are cheque numbers.
   (ii) Debits are withdrawals from the account and Credits are deposits in the account.
   (iii) The dates shown in the Cash Book differ from those in the Bank Statement indicating the time taken for the transactions to be recorded by the bank.

3. Bank Reconciliation

The Bank Statement may not agree with the Cash Book for a number of reasons, such as:
(i)   delays in presenting cheques for payment,
(ii) 'Unknown' items, such as bank charges, not having been recorded in the cash book.

The Bank Statement for the account may, therefore, have appeared as follows:

Bank Statement – The National Bank Ltd.				
Date	*Details*	*Debits*	*Credits*	*Balance*
Jan. 1	Balance forward:			254·50
6	920 123	20·00		234·50
13	920 125	50·00		
14	920 124	65·00		119·50
18	920 126	19·28		100·22
19	920 127	40·00		60·22
31	Charges	1·24		58·98
31	Cheque		324·36	383·34

We now see that the 'Bank' balance is different from the Cash Book balance and by careful checking of each item we see:
(i)   that the bank has debited the account with bank charges of £1·24 which are not shown in the Cash Book,
(ii) the cheque for £24·30 (no. 920 128) has not been presented to the bank for payment.

The Reconciliation of the Bank balance and Cash Book balance can now be shown as follows:

	£
Balance as per Bank Statement	383·34
Add: Bank charges not debited in Cash Book	1·24
	384·58
Less: Cheque not presented (920 128)	24·30
Balance as per Cash Book	360·28

4.   Petty Cash Book

Not all items of expenditure in the office can be made by cheque. Frequently cash has to be used for a variety of small items such as fares, stationery and postages. The cashier responsible for Petty Cash will receive a 'float' from which payments are made and periodically, usually once a month, a sum is paid into the petty cash account to restore the balance to its original amount. Petty cash transactions are usually recorded in an analysis book which will give, month by month, an analysis of petty cash expenditure under certain headings.

Example   A business operates a Petty Cash float of £50. During the month of January the following payments were made:

Jan.	2	Stamps	2·50
	4	Laundry	1·15
	6	Fares	2·84
	9	Milk bill	1·90
	12	Stationery	1·20
	13	Window cleaner	1·80
	16	Fares	2·75
	19	Traveller's expenses	2·30
	23	Office milk bill	1·72
	26	Envelopes	0·68
	27	Stamps	12·40
	29	Fares	1·24

These payments can then be recorded as follows, using the heading: Postages, Cleaning, Stationery, Fares, Office expenses.

Petty Cash Book

Date	Details	Total	Date	Details	V.N.	Total	Postages	Cleaning	Stationery	Fares	Office expenses
		£				£	£	£	£	£	£
Jan. 1	Cash	50·00	Jan. 2	Stamps	1	2·50	2·50				
			" 4	Laundry	2	1·15		1·15			
			" 6	Fares	3	2·84				2·84	
			" 9	Milk	4	1·90					1·90
			" 12	Stationery	5	1·20			1·20		
			" 13	Window cleaner	6	1·80		1·80			
			" 16	Fares	7	2·75				2·75	
			" 19	Traveller's expenses	8	2·30				2·30	
			" 23	Milk	9	1·72					1·72
			" 26	Envelopes	10	0·68			0·68		
			" 27	Stamps	11	12·40	12·40				
			" 29	Fares	12	1·24				1·24	
						32·48	14·90	2·95	1·88	9·13	3·62
		£50·00	" 31	Balance c/d		17·52					
						£50·00					
Feb. 1	Balance	17·52									
" 1	Cash	32·48									

Note: The number in the column V.N. is the Voucher Number which gives details of the payment.

5.   Assignments G

1.   To write up a Cash Book and calculate balance at end of period.

Data:	*Date*		*Transaction*	£
	Mar.	1	Balance	236·40
		2	Cashed cheque	30·00
		4	Paid month's rent	80·00
		10	Cashed cheque	25·00
		12	Paid gas bill	15·35
		15	Paid telephone bill	16·20
		20	Paid TV rent	6·40
		21	Cashed cheque	30·00
		24	Received birthday present	20·00
		28	Paid deposit on holiday	45·00
		31	Received salary	320·36

2.   To write up the Cash Book for a Sports Club, verify with Bank Statement and produce bank reconciliation.

Data: (i)	*Date*		*Transaction*	£
	Jul.	1	Balance	536·15
		3	Subscription rcd. (A. Jones)	10·00
		4	Subscription rcd. (E. Harris)	10·00
		5	Wages paid to Groundsman	30·00
		6	Purchase tennis balls	17·50
		12	Club dance (net income)	24·30
		15	Subscription rcd. (M. Reed)	10·00
		22	Rent paid	52·00
		24	Secretarial expenses paid	12·30
		24	Paid for repairs to club house	21·95
		25	Subscription rcd. (S. Barker)	10·00
		26	Subscription rcd. (B. King)	10·00
		27	Cashed cheque for Petty Cash	20·00
		28	Paid entry fee for tournament	15·00

   (ii)   All payments were by cheque.

(iii)   Extract from Bank Statement as follows:

Date	Detail		Debits	Credits	Balance
	Safe Bank Ltd.				
Jul. 1	Balance forward				536·15
8	Cheques			20·00	556·15
10		172 131	30·00		
11		172 132	17·50		508·65
17	Cheque			24·30	532·95
17	Cheque			10·00	542·95
27		172 134	12·30		530·65
29	Cheque			20·00	550·65
30		172 136	20·00		
30		172 133	52·00		478·65
31	Charges		1·40		477·25

3. To draw up a Bank Reconciliation statement.

   Data: (i)   Balance as per Bank Statement 30th June £124·60.

   (ii)   Balance as per Cash Book 30th June £84·55.

   (iii)   Cheque drawn for £52·30, but not presented.

   (iv)   Cheque drawn for £8·15, but not presented.

   (v)   Bank interest charged £8·40, but not shown in Cash Book.

   (vi)   Cheque for £12 paid into bank on 29th June, but not yet credited by bank.

4. To write up and balance a Petty Cash account.

   Data: (i)   'Float' of £30 at commencement of each month.

   (ii)   Analysis headings to be used: Postages, Fares. Cleaning, Stationery, Sundry Expenses.

   (iii)   Petty Cash payments for month.

Date	No.	Detail	£
June 1	1	Stamps	1·50
4	2	Cleaning	2·25
5	3	Sundries	·72
5	4	Fares	3·54
9	5	Fares	2·13
12	6	Envelopes	·86
15	7	Window cleaner	2·50
16	8	Sundries	1·05
22	9	Stationery	1·95
24	10	Stamps	2·20
25	11	Parcel post	1·75
26	12	Fares	1·84

H. Wages and National Insurance

1. Methods of Determining Earnings

An employee's earnings may be assessed in one of several different ways, e.g. as an annual amount, usually referred to as a salary, or on a weekly or hourly basis, when it is usually called a wage. In addition, wages may be related to actual output of work done and include a production bonus. For staff engaged in selling it is a common practice to pay commission calculated as a percentage of total sales.

Example   (i) A man is employed for a 40 hour week at £3·75 per hour. Calculate his weekly wage.

Weekly wage = £3·75 × 40

                = £150

Example   (ii) A person is employed at an annual salary of £5400. How much will he receive each month?

Monthly salary = £5400 ÷ 12

                = £450

Example   (iii) A salesman receives an annual salary of £3600 paid monthly, plus a commission of 5% of the value of his sales. How much will he receive in a month in which he sold goods to the value of £2800?

Salary   = £300 (£3600 ÷ 12)

Commission   = £140 (5% of £2800)

Total earnings = £440

2. Overtime

When workers are employed for more than the standard week it is usual to pay the 'Overtime' at a higher rate. This may be at time plus a quarter or time plus a half. Sometimes, for work on Sundays or Bank Holidays, double time is paid.

Example   A man's standard working week is 40 hours from Monday to Friday. Overtime worked in the evenings is paid at time plus a quarter and Saturday work at double time. His normal rate is £3·24 per hour. How much will he earn in a week in which he works 49 hours, 5 of which were in the evening and 4 on Saturday?

$$
\begin{array}{llll}
 & & & \text{£} \\
\text{Normal work week} & = 3{\cdot}24 \times 40 & = & 129{\cdot}60 \\
\text{Overtime (evenings)} & = 4{\cdot}05 \times 5 & = & 20{\cdot}25 \\
\text{Overtime (Saturday)} & = 6{\cdot}48 \times 4 & = & 25{\cdot}92 \\
\hline
 & & & 175{\cdot}77
\end{array}
$$

3. Deductions from Earnings

The above calculations are 'gross' earnings from which a number of deductions may be made. The most important of these are:

  (i)   Income Tax (see separate Section I).
 (ii)   National Insurance.
(iii)   Superannuation.

Having made these deductions, the final amount or 'net' earnings is the actual amount received by the employee.

Example   A man's monthly salary is £460. If deductions in one month are as follows: Income Tax £86·37, National Insurance £41·40 and Superannuation £23·00, what will his net monthly salary amount to?

		£	£
Cross salary	=		460·00
Less: Income Tax	=	86·37	
National Insurance	=	41·40	
Superannuation	=	23·00	150·77
Net salary	=		309·23

4. National Insurance

National Insurance is a compulsory payment. The contributions are paid into a fund which provides retirement pensions and other social benefits. For most employees National Insurance contributions are set at one of two levels. For those who will have the full benefit of the State Pension scheme, which is a basic pension plus an additional pension based on earnings, the contribution at January 1984 is 9% of gross earnings up to a maximum earnings limit of £250 per week or £1018·33 per month. Employees earning below £34 per week or £147·33 per month pay no National Insurance. Employees who are 'contracted out' of the State Pension scheme will pay 9% of the first £34 per week of gross earnings and 6·85% on the remainder up to the maximum earnings limit, but contracted-out employees receive only a basic pension on retirement. In order to contract out of the State scheme, employees must belong to an occupational pension scheme which provides additional benefits at least as good as those provided by the State scheme.

Example (i) A man earns a gross weekly wage of £172. He pays the full National Insurance contribution of 9%. What will be the weekly deduction for N.I.?

$$\text{National Insurance} = £\frac{9}{100} \times \frac{172}{1}$$
$$= £15·48$$

Example (ii) A man receives a monthly salary of £330. He is contracted out of the State pension scheme and pays National Insurance at the reduced rate. What will his monthly NI. contribution be?

	£	£
Monthly salary	330·00	
N.I. at 9% on	147·33	= 13·26
N.I. at 6·85% on	182·67	= 12·51
Total N.I. for month		= £25·77

5. Superannuation

In addition to the State pension scheme many firms, industries and other organisations provide pensions for their employees through their own 'Occupational' pension schemes. These schemes usually relate pensions to length of service and actual earnings at time of retirement. Occupational pension schemes usually provide pensions of one-half to one-third of final earnings and contributions are of the order of 5–6% of earnings.

6. Assignments H

1. To calculate the weekly gross pay for an hourly paid worker, his deductions and net pay.

    Data: (i)   Normal hours 8.00–12.00 and 13.00–17.00 Monday–Friday.

    (ii)   If overtime is worked there is a tea-break from 17.00 to 17.30 and overtime is paid from 17.30.

    (iii) Five minutes is allowed for lateness, after which deductions for lost time are made in quarter hours.

    (iv)   Hourly rate of pay is £3·20.

    (v)   Overtime is paid at time plus a quarter.

(vi)

TIME CARD	–	J. SMITH		
Day	In	Out	In	Out
Mon.	8.00	12.00	13.00	17.00
Tues.	7.50	12.01	13.01	19.30
Wed.	7.55	12.02	13.03	19.00
Thurs.	8.02	12.01	13.01	19.30
Fri.	8.22	12.00	12.59	17.01

   (vi)   Income tax deduction £17·30.
  (viii) N.I. 9% of total pay.

2. To calculate the monthly gross and net salary for a salaried employee.

   Data: (i)   Annual salary £7260.
          (ii) Income tax for month £81·15.
         (iii) National Insurance paid at annual rate of 9% on first £1768 of earnings and 6·85% of remainder.
        (iv) Occupational pension scheme deduction of 6% of salary.

3. To prepare a statement showing gross earnings and N.I. contributions for group of sales assistants who are paid a basic wage plus commission on sales.

   Data: (i)   Commission paid is 2½% of sales.
         (ii) N.I. contribution is 9% of gross earnings.
       (iii) List of employees:

Name	Weekly wage	Sales
Miss Brown	£37·50	£430
Miss White	£51·75	£456
Miss Black	£53·00	£600
Miss Green	£63·40	£484

4. To prepare a statement showing (i) average monthly gross and net earnings for a salesman paid on a salary plus commission basis and (ii) net earnings expressed as a percentage of gross earnings:

Data: (i) Annual salary £5000.
     (ii) Commission 2½% on sales over £3000 per year plus a further bonus of 1¼% on sales over £24 000 per year.
    (iii) National Insurance at 9% of gross earnings.
    (iv) Sales for the year £45 800.
    (v) Income Tax for year £630.

5. To prepare a table showing gross and net weekly earnings for a number of hourly-paid canteen staff.

Data: (i)

Employee	Rate of pay	Hours worked	Income tax
A	£2·30	30	£10·40
B	£2·25	24	£6·48
C	£2·25	22	£6·32
D	£2·18	26	£3·15
E	£2·15	18	—

    (ii) National Insurance at 9% also to be deducted.

I. Income tax

Income Tax is the largest source of revenue for the Government, and affects to some degree nearly every working person in the country. The tax payable is assessed by the Inland Revenue. The payment of Income Tax for most people is by deduction from Wages or Salaries. This method of payment is known as PAYE or 'Pay as you earn'.

The rate of tax payable may vary from year to year, and any changes in the rate are usually announced at the time the Chancellor introduces his Budget to Parliament.

1. Tax Allowances

Income Tax is only paid on part of one's income. From the total income certain allowances are deducted before arriving at the taxable income. These allowances may also change from year to year. Some of the allowances for the year 1983/84 were as follows:

Personal allowance (single person)	£1785
Personal allowance (married person)	£2795
Wife's earned income allowance	£1785
Dependent relative	£100
Expenses, as agreed with Inland Revenue	

If in addition to a wage or salary a person receives certain other forms of income, these are also taken into account when calculating taxable income by making deductions from the allowances due. A statement showing these allowances is issued to each taxpayer annually. This statement is called a Notice of Coding. A simplified Notice of Coding is set out in the following example.

Example   Mr Brown earns a salary of £8400. He is married. He receives an allowance of £40 for expenses relating to his employment, and an allowance of £100 for a dependent relative. In addition to his salary he receives interest from savings, of which £85 are taxable.

The following shows how his Notice of Coding would be made up.

NOTICE OF CODING	
CODING ALLOWANCES	**£**
Expenses	40
Building Society interest payable	—
Personal	2795
Wife's earned income	—
Dependent relative	100
TOTAL ALLOWANCES DUE	2935
Less ALLOWANCES GIVEN AGAINST OTHER INCOME	
Untaxed interest	85
National insurance benefits	—
NET ALLOWANCES	2850
Less TAX UNPAID FOR EARLIER YEARS	—
ALLOWANCES GIVEN AGAINST PAY	2850
Your code for 1983/84 is	285 ⁞ H

The code numbers shown on the Notices of Coding are also notified to employers who will then know from tax tables supplied by the

Inland Revenue the appropriate amount of tax to deduct each month from their employees' salaries.

2. Tax Payable

For the year 1983/84 the rate of tax payable was 30% on the first £14 600 of taxable income and progressively higher rates on larger incomes up to 60% on taxable income over £36 000.

Example   Calculate using the figures in the previous example the annual tax payable by Mr Brown, and how much this will amount to per month.

		£
Salary	=	8400
Less allowance given against pay	=	2850
Taxable income	=	5550
Tax payable at 30%	=	1665
Monthly tax £1665 ÷ 12	=	138·75

3. Pay-As-You-Earn (P.A.Y.E.)

Under the P.A.Y.E. scheme employers deduct the appropriate amount of income tax from the salaries and wages of their employees. To do this they have to be notified by the Inland Revenue of the Code Numbers of all their employees, and then by using P.A.Y.E. tables they can determine the amount to deduct each week or each month.

The following are extracts from P.A.Y.E. tables in use during the tax year 1983/84.

Table A gives the 'Free Pay' entitlement for month 1 for code numbers from 0 to 480.

Table B gives the amount of tax due on amounts of taxable pay from £361·00 to £720·00.

MONTH 1
Apr 6 to May 5

TABLE A–FREE PAY

Code	Total free pay to date	Code	Total free pay to date	Code	Total free pay to date	Code	Total free pay to date	Code	Total free pay to date	Code	Total free pay to date	Code	Total free pay to date	Code	Total free pay to date
	£		£		£		£		£		£		£		£
0	NIL	61	51·59	121	101·59	181	151·59	241	201·59	301	251·59	361	301·59	421	351·59
1	1·59	62	52·42	122	102·42	182	152·42	242	202·42	302	252·42	362	302·42	422	352·42
2	2·42	63	53·25	123	103·25	183	153·25	243	203·25	303	253·25	363	303·25	423	353·25
3	3·25	64	54·09	124	104·09	184	154·09	244	204·09	304	254·09	364	304·09	424	354·09
4	4·09	65	54·92	125	104·92	185	154·92	245	204·92	305	254·92	365	304·92	425	354·92
5	4·92														
6	5·75	66	55·75	126	105·75	186	155·75	246	205·75	306	255·75	366	305·75	426	355·75
7	6·59	67	56·59	127	106·59	187	156·59	247	206·59	307	256·59	367	306·59	427	356·59
8	7·42	68	57·42	128	107·42	188	157·42	248	207·42	308	257·42	368	307·42	428	357·42
9	8·25	69	58·25	129	108·25	189	158·25	249	208·25	309	258·25	369	308·25	429	358·25
10	9·09	70	59·09	130	109·09	190	159·09	250	209·09	310	259·09	370	309·09	430	359·09
11	9·92	71	59·92	131	109·92	191	159·92	251	209·92	311	259·92	371	309·92	431	359·92
12	10·75	72	60·75	132	110·75	192	160·75	252	210·75	312	260·75	372	310·75	432	360·75
13	11·59	73	61·59	133	111·59	193	161·59	253	211·59	313	261·59	373	311·59	433	361·59
14	12·42	74	62·42	134	112·42	194	162·42	254	212·42	314	262·42	374	312·42	434	362·42
15	13·25	75	63·25	135	113·25	195	163·25	255	213·25	315	263·25	375	313·25	435	363·25
16	14·09	76	64·09	136	114·09	196	164·09	256	214·09	316	264·09	376	314·09	436	364·09
17	14·92	77	64·92	137	114·92	197	164·92	257	214·92	317	264·92	377	314·92	437	364·92
18	15·75	78	65·75	138	115·75	198	165·75	258	215·75	318	265·75	378	315·75	438	365·75
19	16·59	79	66·59	139	116·59	199	166·59	259	216·59	319	266·59	379	316·59	439	366·59
20	17·42	80	67·42	140	117·42	200	167·42	260	217·42	320	267·42	380	317·42	440	367·42
21	18·25	81	68·25	141	118·25	201	168·25	261	218·25	321	268·25	381	318·25	441	368·25
22	19·09	82	69·09	142	119·09	202	169·09	262	219·09	322	269·09	382	319·09	442	369·09
23	19·92	83	69·92	143	119·92	203	169·92	263	219·92	323	269·92	383	319·92	443	369·92
24	20·75	84	70·75	144	120·75	204	170·75	264	220·75	324	270·75	384	320·75	444	370·75
25	21·59	85	71·59	145	121·59	205	171·59	265	221·59	325	271·59	385	321·59	445	371·59
26	22·42	86	72·42	146	122·42	206	172·42	266	222·42	326	272·42	386	322·42	446	372·42
27	23·25	87	73·25	147	123·25	207	173·25	267	223·25	327	273·25	387	323·25	447	373·25
28	24·09	88	74·09	148	124·09	208	174·09	268	224·09	328	274·09	388	324·09	448	374·09
29	24·92	89	74·92	149	124·92	209	174·92	269	224·92	329	274·92	389	324·92	449	374·92
30	25·75	90	75·75	150	125·75	210	175·75	270	225·75	330	275·75	390	325·75	450	375·75
31	26·59	91	76·59	151	126·59	211	176·59	271	226·59	331	276·59	391	326·59	451	376·59
32	27·42	92	77·42	152	127·42	212	177·42	272	227·42	332	277·42	392	327·42	452	377·42
33	28·25	93	78·25	153	128·25	213	178·25	273	228·25	333	278·25	393	328·25	453	378·25
34	29·09	94	79·09	154	129·09	214	179·09	274	229·09	334	279·09	394	329·09	454	379·09
35	29·92	95	79·92	155	129·92	215	179·92	275	229·92	335	279·92	395	329·92	455	379·92
36	30·75	96	80·75	156	130·75	216	180·75	276	230·75	336	280·75	396	330·75	456	380·75
37	31·59	97	81·59	157	131·59	217	181·59	277	231·59	337	281·59	397	331·59	457	381·59
38	32·42	98	82·42	158	132·42	218	182·42	278	232·42	338	282·42	398	332·42	458	382·42
39	33·25	99	83·25	159	133·25	219	183·25	279	233·25	339	283·25	399	333·25	459	383·25
40	34·09	100	84·09	160	134·09	220	184·09	280	234·09	340	284·09	400	334·09	460	384·09
41	34·92	101	84·92	161	134·92	221	184·92	281	234·92	341	284·92	401	334·92	461	384·92
42	35·75	102	85·75	162	135·75	222	185·75	282	235·75	342	285·75	402	335·75	462	385·75
43	36·59	103	86·59	163	136·59	223	186·59	283	236·59	343	286·59	403	336·59	463	386·59
44	37·42	104	87·42	164	137·42	224	187·42	284	237·42	344	287·42	404	337·42	464	387·42
45	38·25	105	88·25	165	138·25	225	188·25	285	238·25	345	288·25	405	338·25	465	388·25
46	39·09	106	89·09	166	139·09	226	189·09	286	239·09	346	289·09	406	339·09	466	389·09
47	39·92	107	89·92	167	139·92	227	189·92	287	239·92	347	289·92	407	339·92	467	389·92
48	40·75	108	90·75	168	140·75	228	190·75	288	240·75	348	290·75	408	340·75	468	390·75
49	41·59	109	91·59	169	141·59	229	191·59	289	241·59	349	291·59	409	341·59	469	391·59
50	42·42	110	92·42	170	142·42	230	192·42	290	242·42	350	292·42	410	342·42	470	392·42
51	43·25	111	93·25	171	143·25	231	193·25	291	243·25	351	293·25	411	343·25	471	393·25
52	44·09	112	94·09	172	144·09	232	194·09	292	244·09	352	294·09	412	344·09	472	394·09
53	44·92	113	94·92	173	144·92	233	194·92	293	244·92	353	294·92	413	344·92	473	394·92
54	45·75	114	95·75	174	145·75	234	195·75	294	245·75	354	295·75	414	345·75	474	395·75
55	46·59	115	96·59	175	146·59	235	196·59	295	246·59	355	296·59	415	346·59	475	396·59
56	47·42	116	97·42	176	147·42	236	197·42	296	247·42	356	297·42	416	347·42	476	397·42
57	48·25	117	98·25	177	148·25	237	198·25	297	248·25	357	298·25	417	348·25	477	398·25
58	49·09	118	99·09	178	149·09	238	199·09	298	249·09	358	299·09	418	349·09	478	399·09
59	49·92	119	99·92	179	149·92	239	199·92	299	249·92	359	299·92	419	349·92	479	399·92
60	50·75	120	100·75	180	150·75	240	200·75	300	250·75	360	300·75	420	350·75	480	400·75

TABLE B

TAX DUE ON TAXABLE PAY FROM £361 TO £720

Total TAXABLE PAY to date	Total TAX DUE to date	Total TAXABLE PAY to date	Total TAX DUE to date	Total TAXABLE PAY to date	Total TAX DUE to date	Total TAXABLE PAY to date	Total TAX DUE to date	Total TAXABLE PAY to date	Total TAX DUE to date	Total TAXABLE PAY to date	Total TAX DUE to date
£	£	£	£	£	£	£	£	£	£	£	£
361	108.30	421	126.30	481	144.30	541	162.30	601	180.30	661	198.30
362	108.60	422	126.60	482	144.60	542	162.60	602	180.60	662	198.60
363	108.90	423	126.90	483	144.90	543	162.90	603	180.90	663	198.90
364	109.20	424	127.20	484	145.20	544	163.20	604	181.20	664	199.20
365	109.50	425	127.50	485	145.50	545	163.50	605	181.50	665	199.50
366	109.80	426	127.80	486	145.80	546	163.80	606	181.80	666	199.80
367	110.10	427	128.10	487	146.10	547	164.10	607	182.10	667	200.10
368	110.40	428	128.40	488	146.40	548	164.40	608	182.40	668	200.40
369	110.70	429	128.70	489	146.70	549	164.70	609	182.70	669	200.70
370	111.00	430	129.00	490	147.00	550	165.00	610	183.00	670	201.00
371	111.30	431	129.30	491	147.30	551	165.30	611	183.30	671	201.30
372	111.60	432	129.60	492	147.60	552	165.60	612	183.60	672	201.60
373	111.90	433	129.90	493	147.90	553	165.90	613	183.90	673	201.90
374	112.20	434	130.20	494	148.20	554	166.20	614	184.20	674	202.20
375	112.50	435	130.50	495	148.50	555	166.50	615	184.50	675	202.50
376	112.80	436	130.80	496	148.80	556	166.80	616	184.80	676	202.80
377	113.10	437	131.10	497	149.10	557	167.10	617	185.10	677	203.10
378	113.40	438	131.40	498	149.40	558	167.40	618	185.40	678	203.40
379	113.70	439	131.70	499	149.70	559	167.70	619	185.70	679	203.70
380	114.00	440	132.00	500	150.00	560	168.00	620	186.00	680	204.00
381	114.30	441	132.30	501	150.30	561	168.30	621	186.30	681	204.30
382	114.60	442	132.60	502	150.60	562	168.60	622	186.60	682	204.60
383	114.90	443	132.90	503	150.90	563	168.90	623	186.90	683	204.90
384	115.20	444	133.20	504	151.20	564	169.20	624	187.20	684	205.20
385	115.50	445	133.50	505	151.50	565	169.50	625	187.50	685	205.50
386	115.80	446	133.80	506	151.80	566	169.80	626	187.80	686	205.80
387	116.10	447	134.10	507	152.10	567	170.10	627	188.10	687	206.10
388	116.40	448	134.40	508	152.40	568	170.40	628	188.40	688	206.40
389	116.70	449	134.70	509	152.70	569	170.70	629	188.70	689	206.70
390	117.00	450	135.00	510	153.00	570	171.00	630	189.00	690	207.00
391	117.30	451	135.30	511	153.30	571	171.30	631	189.30	691	207.30
392	117.60	452	135.60	512	153.60	572	171.60	632	189.60	692	207.60
393	117.90	453	135.90	513	153.90	573	171.90	633	189.90	693	207.90
394	118.20	454	136.20	514	154.20	574	172.20	634	190.20	694	208.20
395	118.50	455	136.50	515	154.50	575	172.50	635	190.50	695	208.50
396	118.80	456	136.80	516	154.80	576	172.80	636	190.80	696	208.80
397	119.10	457	137.10	517	155.10	577	173.10	637	191.10	697	209.10
398	119.40	458	137.40	518	155.40	578	173.40	638	191.40	698	209.40
399	119.70	459	137.70	519	155.70	579	173.70	639	191.70	699	209.70
400	120.00	460	138.00	520	156.00	580	174.00	640	192.00	700	210.00
401	120.30	461	138.30	521	156.30	581	174.30	641	192.30	701	210.30
402	120.60	462	138.60	522	156.60	582	174.60	642	192.60	702	210.60
403	120.90	463	138.90	523	156.90	583	174.90	643	192.90	703	210.90
404	121.20	464	139.20	524	157.20	584	175.20	644	133.20	704	211.20
405	121.50	465	139.50	525	157.50	585	175.50	645	193.50	705	211.50
406	121.80	466	139.80	526	157.80	586	175.80	646	193.80	706	211.80
407	122.10	467	140.10	527	158.10	587	176.10	647	194.10	707	212.10
408	122.40	468	140.40	528	158.40	588	176.40	648	194.40	708	212.40
409	122.70	469	140.70	529	158.70	589	176.70	649	194.70	709	212.70
410	123.00	470	141.00	530	159.00	590	177.00	650	195.00	710	213.00
411	123.30	471	141.30	531	159.30	591	177.30	651	195.30	711	213.30
412	123.60	472	141.60	532	159.60	592	177.60	652	195.60	712	213.60
413	123.90	473	141.90	533	159.90	593	177.90	653	195.90	713	213.90
414	124.20	474	142.20	534	160.20	594	178.20	654	196.20	714	214.20
415	124.50	475	142.50	535	160.50	595	178.50	655	196.50	715	214.50
416	124.80	476	142.80	536	160.80	596	178.80	656	196.80	716	214.80
417	125.10	477	143.10	537	161.10	597	179.10	657	197.10	717	215.10
418	125.40	478	143.40	538	161.40	598	179.40	658	197.40	718	215.40
419	125.70	479	143.70	539	161.70	599	179.70	659	197.70	719	215.70
420	126.00	480	144.00	540	162.00	600	180.00	660	198.00	720	216.00

To illustrate the use of these tables we can use the example in the previous section.

First look at Table A for Code No. 285 and we see that the month's free-pay entitlement is £238·25. This amount is approximately one-twelfth of £2850 – the allowances given against pay for the whole year.

Having determined the free-pay for the month the taxable pay is calculated by subtracting free pay from gross pay:

$$
\begin{array}{lr}
 & \text{£} \\
\text{Gross pay £8400} \div 12 & = 700{\cdot}00 \\
\text{Free pay} & = \underline{238{\cdot}25} \\
 & \\
\text{Taxable pay} & = 461{\cdot}75
\end{array}
$$

Now turn to Table B and we find the tax due on £462·00 (the nearest amount shown) is £138·60. There is a slight discrepancy between the calculated monthly tax of £138·75 and the amount shown in the tables. These discrepancies arise because any one code number covers a range of tax allowances of £10. For instance, code number 285 covers persons with tax allowances from £2850 to £2859. The small adjustments in tax due are made at the end of the tax year.

4. Assignments I

1. To calculate a person's monthly tax liability.

   Data: (i)   Annual salary £6320.
   (ii)   Allowances to set against pay £2145.
   (iii)   Rate of tax payable 30%.

2. To estimate a person's weekly tax liability and the percentage of gross earnings he pays in tax.

   Data: (i)   Earnings 40 hours a week at £2·75 per hour.
   (ii)   Annual earnings to be based on the same weekly earnings for 52 weeks.
   (iii)   Allowances to be set against pay for the year £1785.
   (iv)   Tax to be calculated at 30%.

3. To calculate a man's monthly tax liability and percentage of gross salary paid in tax:

   Data: (i) Annual salary £7560.
   - (ii) Use allowances shown in text.
   - (iii) Married person's allowance is claimed.
   - (iv) Expenses allowed £35.
   - (v) Dependent relative allowance claimed.
   - (vi) He receives an additional income of £60 on which tax has to be paid.
   - (vii) Tax payable at 30%.

4. To prepare a Notice of Coding.
   Data: (i) Use allowances shown in text.
   - (ii) A married person's allowance is claimed.
   - (iii) Taxable interest of £55 is received.
   - (iv) Expenses of £60 allowed.
   - (v) Dependent relative allowance claimed.

5. To determine the amount of tax payable for one month using tax tables and to verify this amount by calculation.
   Data: (i) Tax payable relates to month 1 of tax year.
   - (ii) Annual salary received £6480.
   - (iii) Allowances to set against pay £1785.
   - (iv) Use section of tables shown in text.
   - (v) Tax is payable at 30%.

J. Buying and selling – prices, profits and discounts

1. Prices, Mark-up or Margin

To arrive at the selling price of his goods a shopkeeper will add a profit margin on to their cost price. The profit margin, sometimes known as gross profit or mark-up, must be sufficient to cover the operating costs of running the business. Profit margins are usually calculated as a percentage of the selling price.

Example   Cost price of article $= £7$
Profit margin required $= 30\%$ of S.P.

$$\text{Then selling price} = \text{C.P.} \times \frac{100}{100-30}$$

$$= £7 \times \frac{100}{70} = £10$$

i.e. Actual profit $= £10 - £7 = £3$

and Profit as $\%$ of S.P. $\dfrac{3}{10} \times \dfrac{100}{1} = 30\%$

2. Prices, Recommended by Manufacturer

Some manufacturers produce a list of goods that they are marketing together with their recommended retail prices. These goods are then sold to the shopkeeper at list price less a substantial trade discount. If the retailer then sells the goods at the recommended price the trade discount equals the profit margin to the retailer.

£

Example List Price of article $\qquad= 72$
    Less: Trade Discount $33\frac{1}{3}\% = 24$

    Invoiced price to retailer $\quad= 48$

£

    Retailer's Selling Price $\quad= 72$
    Retailer's Cost Price $\qquad= 48$

    Profit $\qquad\qquad\qquad= 24$

    Profit as % of S.P. $\qquad = \dfrac{24}{72} \times \dfrac{100}{1} = 33\frac{1}{3}\%$

3. Prices, Mark-down

At 'Sale' time prices of goods are reduced with a view to clearing old stock. This price reduction is known as the mark-down. Mark-downs are usually calculated as a percentage of the normal selling price.

4. Cash Discounts

Cash discounts are offered to encourage prompt payment of accounts. The terms of the discount are usually shown on the invoice, e.g. Terms $2\frac{1}{2}\%$ one month, which means that $2\frac{1}{2}\%$ may be deducted from the invoiced price of the goods provided the account is settled within one month. Although cash discounts appear small, it must be remembered that $2\frac{1}{2}\%$ for one month is equivalent to an annual rate of interest of $30\% (2\frac{1}{2} \times 12)$. Cash discounts are deductible from the invoiced price after any trade discount has been allowed. In the previous example the Cash Discount would be calculated as follows:

£

List Price $\qquad\qquad\qquad\qquad = 72 \cdot 00$
Less: Trade Discount $33\frac{1}{3}\% \qquad = 24 \cdot 00$

Invoiced Price $\qquad\qquad\qquad = 48 \cdot 00$
Less: Cash Discount $2\frac{1}{2}\% \qquad\quad = \ 1 \cdot 20$

Amount paid in settlement of account $= 46 \cdot 80$

5. Value Added Tax (V.A.T.)

To simplify the above examples V.A.T. has been disregarded. This is a tax that is added at the time of sale to many goods and services. The current rate of tax on most goods is 15%. Some goods, however, are zero-rated and others exempt from tax. Food, water, fuel and power are examples of zero-rated goods: postal services, insurance and education are examples of services which are exempt. Although, from a calculations point of view, there is no difference between zero-rating and exemption, there is, nevertheless, an important distinction between the two to be made when determining overall tax liability.

A business will pay V.A.T. on the goods it purchases, and then charge V.A.T. on the goods it sells. Careful records have to be kept of all these transactions, and the difference between the tax charged to customers and the tax payable to suppliers is the net amount actually paid over to Customs and Excise. V.A.T. is chargeable on the discounted price of goods.

Using the figures from the previous example we get:

	£
List Price of article	= 72·00
Less: Trade Discount 33⅓%	= 24·00
Invoiced Price to retailer	= 48·00
Plus: V.A.T. at 15%	= 7·20
Amount paid by retailer	=55·20
Retailer's Selling Price	=72·00
Plus: V.A.T. at 15%	=10·80
Amount charged to customer	= 82·80
V.A.T. collected by retailer	=10·80
V.A.T. paid by retailer	= 7·20
V.A.T. paid over to Customs and Excise	= 3·60

6. The Invoice

The Invoice is a business document setting out the details of goods purchased by a customer, including the price charged for the goods, any discounts allowed, V.A.T. payable and any special terms relating to payment. The following is an example of an Invoice:

INVOICE No. 2345

R. W. BROWN LTD.
WESTMEAD TRADING ESTATE, SHEFFIELD

TO: D.I.Y. TOOLS LTD.   Date: 1 AUG. 1983
     HIGH STREET   Order No.: 247G
     LONDON E6.

Quantity	Description	Unit Price (£)	Amount (£)
10	Chisels	1·25	12·50
20	Folding rules	1·40	28·00
20	Hammers	2·80	56·00
15	Planes	5·40	81·00
50	Screwdrivers	·95	47·50
	Total		225·00
	Less: Trade Discount $33\frac{1}{3}\%$		75·00
			150·00
	Plus: V.A.T. 15%		22·50
			172·50

7.   Gross Profit – the Trading Account

From time to time a business will need to prepare a statement of accounts which shows its trading position. In the case of a small retail business a trading account showing gross profit can be prepared from figures giving total sales and cost of goods sold. To get this latter figure, however, a valuation of stock at the beginning and end of the trading period must be made. This is done by an actual count of the stock or 'stock-taking'. Its value is then determined at cost price.

8.   Net Profit – the Profit and Loss Account

To get a true picture of the profitability of a business it is necessary to deduct from the Gross Profit the Operating Expenses of the business. These will include such items as rent, salaries, heating and lighting, telephones, transport, etc. Gross Profit less Operating Expenses will give the Net Profit.

A combined Trading and Profit and Loss Account may be prepared as follows:

A. B. Smith & Co.
Trading and Profit & Loss Account for the month ended 31st Jan. 1984.

	£	£
Sales		2950
Cost of goods sold		
Stock, 1 Jan.	575	
Add: Purchases in Jan.	1595	
Goods available for sale	2170	
Less: Stock 31 Jan.	425	1745
Gross profit on sales		1205
Operating expenses		
Rent	160	
Salaries	520	
Heating and lighting	55	
General expenses	110	845
Net profit for month		360

9. Assignments J

1. To prepare an invoice from given data.

   Data: (i) Names of supplier and purchaser fictitious.
   (ii) List of items to be invoiced:
   20 reams of paper at £1·75 ream.
   1500 envelopes at 86p per 100.
   8 boxes carbon paper at £4·32 per box.
   50 notebooks at 24p each.
   120 pencils at 7p each.
   150 biro pens at 11½p each.
   (iii) Trade Discount of 25% to be deducted.
   (iv) V.A.T. at 15% to be added.

2. To prepare a list showing the Selling Price of a number of items, given their Cost Price and percentage profit margin.

   Data: (i) Profit margin to be 27½% of Selling Price calculated to nearest penny.

(ii) *Items listed*	*Cost Price*
Shirts	£4·25
Ties	£1·20
Socks	£0·85
Singlets	£1·35
Handkerchiefs	£1·30

3. To determine the net price of goods charged by a manufacturer to a retailer, given List Price, Trade Discount and V.A.T.

Data: (i) *Items*	*List Price*
Table	£56·75
Chairs	£24·30
Sideboard	£86·40
Settee suite	£495·00

   (ii) Trade Discount 33⅓%.
   (iii) V.A.T. 15%.

4. To calculate the gross profit on a list of goods, given their Selling Price and percentage Profit Margin.

Data: *S.P. of goods*   *Gross Profit as % of S.P.*
             Item A £4·36   25%
                  B £3·69   33⅓%
                  C £5·60   17½%
                  D £1·99   20%
                  E £3·74   22½%

5.   To calculate the 'Sale' Price of list of goods, given % mark-down.

Data: (i)   Mark-down 15% of normal selling price.
         (ii) *Items*   *Normal Selling Price*
               Lawnmower 14 in.   £71·50
               Lawnmower 17 in.   £126·40
               Hedge clippers   £16·95
               Edging tool   £24·50
               Lawn roller   £21·30

6.   To prepare a Trading and Profit & Loss Account to show both Gross Profit and Net Profit.

Data: (i)   Account to be for period of one month.
         (ii)   Stock at beginning of month   £894
         (iii) Stock at end of month   £1145
         (iv)   Sales for month   £3692
         (v)   Purchases for month   £2750
         (vi)   Operating expenses for month
                Wages   £360
                Rent   £280
                Heating and lighting   £ 64
                Postage and telephones   £ 13
                Other general expenses   £194

K. Bank loans and hire purchase

1. ## Bank Personal Loans

   Nowadays an increasingly large number of people use bank accounts and are paid their wages or salaries by cheque or bank transfer. Where customers are 'credit-worthy' banks are usually prepared to lend them money for certain purposes. The bank calculates the interest payable on the full loan for the whole period of repayment and the loan plus interest is usually repaid in monthly instalments.

   Example A man wishes to borrow £240 from his bank for home improvement. The bank agrees to the loan with interest at 12% per annum and that repayments will be in 24 monthly instalments. What will be the amount of each instalment?

   $$
   \begin{aligned}
   &\text{Loan} && \pounds \\
   &\text{Loan} && = 240{\cdot}00 \\
   &\text{Interest} = \frac{12}{100} \times \frac{240}{1} \times \frac{2}{1} &&= 57{\cdot}60 \\
   &\text{Total to repay} && = 297{\cdot}60 \\
   &\therefore \text{Each instalment} && = \frac{297{\cdot}60}{24} = \pounds12{\cdot}40
   \end{aligned}
   $$

2. ## Hire Purchase

   Hire Purchase is the term commonly used for the purchase of goods by instalments. The purchaser usually is required to pay a deposit at the time of purchase and the balance of the purchase price plus interest is repaid in a number of instalments. It is usually difficult to say what the true rate of interest amounts to because repayments are by instalments. However, shops frequently work out the interest to be paid by calculating it on the initial balance for the whole period of the repayment.

Example   A shopper buys a piece of furniture for £120. A deposit of $33\frac{1}{3}\%$ is paid and interest at $12\frac{1}{2}\%$ is charged on the outstanding balance for the period of repayment. The balance plus interest is paid in 24 monthly instalments. How much will each instalment be?

$$
\begin{array}{lr}
& \text{£} \\
\text{Price of furniture} & = 120 \\
\textit{Less: } \text{Deposit } 33\frac{1}{3}\% & = 40 \\
\hline
\text{Balance outstanding} & = 80 \\
\textit{Plus: } \text{Interest} = \dfrac{12\frac{1}{2}}{100}\times\dfrac{80}{1}\times\dfrac{2}{1} & = 20 \\
\hline
\text{Amount to be repaid} & = 100 \\
\hline
\end{array}
$$

$\therefore$ Each instalment $= \dfrac{100}{24} = £4 \cdot 17$ (nearest penny)

In this example $12\frac{1}{2}\%$ would be the true rate of interest on this loan if the whole of the £80 balance was not repaid until the end of the two year period, but this is not the case. £80 is only borrowed for 1 month until the first instalment is paid. After that the amount of the loan outstanding is reduced each month, but as the instalments remain the same each month it follows that a bigger proportion of each successive repayment is interest, and hence the rate of interest effectively increases throughout the repayment period.

3.   The True Rate of Interest

The calculation of the true rate of interest is very complicated and outside the scope of this book, but the following example illustrates how the true rate differs from the rate of interest when calculated using the method in the previous example. It can be shown that a loan of £300 at 10% p.a. interest can be repaid in three equal annual instalments of £121 (calculated to the nearest £). The variations in the interest and loan repayments in each instalment would be as follows:

	Loan repayment		*Interest*		*Total instalment*
End of 1st Year	91	+	30	=	121
End of 2nd Year	100	+	21	=	121
End of 3rd Year	109	+	12	=	121
	£300		£63		£363

The interest charged on this loan over a three year period is £63. If then we calculate the rate of interest based on the intial loan of £300 using the S.I. formula we get:

$$R = \frac{100}{P} \times \frac{I}{N} \qquad \text{where } I = £63$$
$$= \frac{100 \times 63}{300 \times 3} \% \qquad P = £300$$
$$= 7\% \qquad N = 3 \text{ yrs.}$$

In this example we see that the rate of interest based on the initial loan is 7%, but the true rate of interest is 10%.

4. The 'Average' Loan

Although calculations involving the true rate of interest are necessary when dealing with long-term loans such as mortgages, they are unnecessarily complex for the average H.P. transaction. For these transactions a reasonably true rate of interest can be determined by calculating the 'average' loan for the repayment period as the following example shows:

Example (i) A man buys a secondhand car for £160. He pays a deposit of £40. The balance plus interest at 15% on this balance for the whole period of repayment is to be repaid in 4 equal quarterly instalments. What is the rate of interest charged when calculated on the 'average' loan?

	£
Price of car	= 160·00
Less Deposit	= 40·00
Balance outstanding	= 120·00
Plus interest at 15% for 1 year	= 18·00
	138·00

$$\therefore \text{ Each Instalment } = \frac{138\cdot00}{4} = £34\cdot50$$

But £120 is not borrowed for the whole year. If we assume that of each instalment £30 is repayment of the loan and £4·50 is interest, then

£120 is the loan outstanding only for the first 3 months
£90 is the loan outstanding for the next 3 months
£60 is the loan outstanding for the next 3 months
and £30 is the loan outstanding for the final 3 months
$\therefore$ The average amount of the loan for the whole year

$$\frac{120+90+60+30}{4} = \frac{300}{4} = £75$$

If then £18 interest is charged on a loan of £75 for 1 year the rate of interest charged is obtained from the formula:

$$R = \frac{100 \times I}{P \times N}$$
$$= \frac{100 \times 18}{75 \times 1} \%$$
$$= \frac{1800}{75} = \underline{24\%}$$

where I = £18
P = £75
N = 1 year

Example (ii) An article is advertised for sale at £25 cash or by a deposit of £5 and 10 monthly instalments of £2·20. What was the rate of interest charged when

(i) calculated on the 'average' loan.
and (ii) calculated on the 'initial' loan?

$$
\begin{array}{lcr}
 & & \text{£} \\
\text{Cash Price} & = & 25 \\
\text{Deposit} & = & 5 \\
\hline
\text{Balance outstanding} & = & 20 \\
\text{(the initial loan)} & & \\
\text{Repayments £2·20} \times 10 & = & 22 \\
\text{Repayment of loan} & = & 20 \\
\hline
\text{Interest paid} & = & \text{£2}
\end{array}
$$

It is assumed that each instalment comprises £2 repayment of loan and £0·20 interest.

∴ £20 is borrowed for 1 month
£18 is borrowed for 1 month
£16 is borrowed for 1 month
£14 is borrowed for 1 month
etc.,
£2 is borrowed for 1 month
and the average loan

$$
= \frac{£20+18+16+14+12+10+8+6+4+2}{10}
$$

$$
= \frac{£110}{10} = £11
$$

(i) Rate of interest based on 'Average' Loan

$$
\begin{aligned}
R &= \frac{100 \times I}{P \times N} \qquad \text{where } I = £2 \\
 & \qquad\qquad\qquad\quad P = £11 \\
 &= \frac{100 \times 2}{11 \times \frac{10}{12}} \qquad\quad N = \tfrac{10}{12} \text{ yr.} \\
 &= \frac{240}{11} = 21\!\cdot\!82\%
\end{aligned}
$$

(ii)   Rate of interest based on 'Initial' Loan

$$R = \frac{100 \times I}{P \times N} \qquad \text{where } I = £2$$
$$\qquad\qquad\qquad\qquad P = £20$$
$$= \frac{100 \times 2}{20 \times \frac{10}{12}} \qquad\qquad N = \tfrac{10}{12} \text{ yr.}$$
$$= 12\%$$

Note. The numbers 20, 18, 16, ... 2 form a series known as an arithmetic progression, a series in which there is a common difference between the terms in the series. The sum of an A.P. can be found by using the formula:

$$\text{Sum} = \frac{n}{2}(a+1) \text{ Where } n = \text{ the no. of terms in the series}$$
$$a = \text{ the first term}$$
$$\text{and } 1 = \text{ the last term}$$

In the series shown n = 10 (i.e. the number of payments)
$$a = 20$$
$$1 = 2$$
$$\therefore S = \frac{10}{2}(20+2) = 5 \times 22 = £110$$

Example   (iii)   An article is advertised for sale at £13 cash or by instalments with a deposit of £2·56 and 6 monthly payments of £1·82. What is the rate of interest being charged? (Calculate this on the average balance outstanding after the deposit is paid.)

		£
Cash price	=	13·00
Less deposit	=	2·56
Balance outstanding	=	10·44
Repayments 6 × £1·82	=	10·92
Less balance outstanding	=	10·44
∴ Interest paid on loan	=	0·48

$$\text{Rate of interest} = \frac{100 \times I}{P \times N}$$

$$= \frac{100 \times 0.48}{6.09 \times 0.5}\%$$

$$= \frac{48}{3.045} = \underline{15.8\%}$$

where $I = £0.48$

$P = £6.09*$

$N = 0.5$ years

$*S = 3(10.44 + 1.74)$

$= £36.54$

$\therefore P = \frac{£36.54}{6} = \underline{\underline{£6.09}}$

5. Assignments K

1. To calculate the repayment instalments on a bank personal loan when interest is calculated on the 'initial' loan, and to determine what rate of interest this represents when calculated on the 'average' loan.

   Data: (i) Amount of loan £360.

   (ii) Rate of interest on initial loan $12\frac{1}{2}\%$.

   (iii) Repayments in 36 monthly instalments.

2. To calculate the repayment instalments on a hire purchase deal.

   Data: (i) Cash price of article £84.

   (ii) Deposit paid 25%.

   (iii) Repayments over 24 months.

   (iv) Rate of interest 15% based on the intial loan for the full repayment period.

3. To calculate the rate of interest on a hire purchase transaction when based on (i) the 'initial' loan and (ii) the 'average' loan.

   Data: (i) Cash price of article £66.99.

   (ii) Deposit £7.50.

   (iii) Repayments 9 monthly instalments of £7.45 each.

4. To compare the rate of interest charged on a H.P. deal if calculated on the balance outstanding at the time of the purchase, and if calculated on 'average' loan throughout the period of repayment.

   Data: (i) Cash price of suite of furniture £247.50.

   (ii) H.P. terms 20% deposit and 18 monthly instalments of £12.65.

5. To calculate the rate of interest on the hire purchase of a secondhand car when calculated on the 'average' loan.

Data: (i)   Cash price of car £720.
       (ii) Deposit $33\frac{1}{3}\%$.
       (iii) Repayment in 24 monthly instalments.
       (iv) Rate of interest charged 20% on balance outstanding at time of purchase over the full repayment period.

L. Car and household expenses

1. Car Expenses

Before a car or other motor vehicle can be used it has to be taxed. This is a legal requirement. This tax, known as the Vehicle Licence, is paid when the vehicle is first registered and the tax has to be renewed periodically. In addition, the vehicle must also be insured – another legal requirement under the Road Traffic Acts, to protect a third party who may be injured in an accident.

In calculating the costs of running a car, tax, insurance, petrol, maintenance and depreciation must all be taken into account to obtain an accurate costing.

Example A secondhand car is bought for £1600, used for 1 year and then sold for £1150. During the year it did 12 000 miles averaging 30 miles per gallon on petrol costing 184 p per gallon. Insurance cost £76·50, tax £85, repairs and maintenance £86. Calculate the total cost of the year's motoring and cost per mile.

		£
Costs: Depreciation	=	450·00
Tax	=	85·00
Insurance	=	76·50
Petrol $£\dfrac{12\ 000}{30} \times \dfrac{184}{100}$	=	736·00
Repairs and maintenance	=	86·00
		1433·50

$$\text{Average cost per mile} = \frac{1433 \cdot 50 \times 100}{12\ 000}\ \text{p}$$
$$= \underline{\underline{11 \cdot 9\ \text{p}}}\ \text{(nearest } \frac{1}{10}\ \text{p)}$$

2. Gas Charges

Gas is charged according to the number of therms used. The gas meter records the number of cubic feet of gas used and this is then converted into therms. The conversion from cubic feet to therms depends on the 'calorific value' of the gas supplied.

Example No. of cu.ft. (in hundreds) supplied = 187
Conversion factor = 1·032
∴ No. of therms = 187 × 1·032
= $\underline{\underline{192 \cdot 98}}$

The charge for gas is usually in two parts: a standing charge, which has to be paid quarterly irrespective of how much gas is used, and a charge per therm used. The 1983 rates for one such tariff are set out below:

Credit tariff
Standing charge per quarter   £9·90
Price per therm   33·5 p

A typical quarterly account for a customer on the Credit Tariff is as follows:

LONDON GAS BOARD					
Meter readings		*Consumption*		*Rate*	*Amount*
Present	*Previous*	*100 cu.ft.*	*Therms*	*p*	*£*
9742	9555	187	192·98	33·5	64·65
			Standing charge		9·90
				Total	74·55

Example The readings on a gas meter at the beginning and end of a quarter were 2766 and 2975, the readings being in hundreds of cu.ft. Using the information contained in the text, calculate (i) the number of therms used and (ii) the cost of gas based on the Credit Tariff.

Present reading = 2975 (100 cu.ft.)
Previous reading = 2766 (100 cu.ft.)
Gas used   = 209 (100 cu.ft.)
No. of therms   = 209 × 1·032
                 = 215·69 therms

Cost of gas   £
    215·69 × 33·5 p = 72·26
    Standing charge = 9.90

    Total   = 82·16

3. Electricity Charges

Electricity is charged according to the number of units used, which is recorded on a meter. A one-kilowatt appliance operating for one hour uses one unit of electricity. The Electricity Boards offer consumers a variety of tariffs to meet their special needs. Examples of two of these tariffs with 1983 rates are as follows:

(i) Domestic Tariff suitable for most householders.
     Quarterly charge   £7·58
     Unit charge   5·01 p per unit

(ii) Night-rate Tariff.
     Quarterly charge   £10·08
     Unit charge day rate   5·01 p per unit
     Unit charge night rate   1·90 p per unit

This tariff is suitable for the household that can use electricity during the night when supply is plentiful. Storage radiators and water-heaters are examples of appliances that can be automatically switched on to operate at night-time to make use of cheap electricity.

Example A consumer uses 2000 units of electricity in one quarter, 800 of which are used at night. Calculate, using the figures quoted in the text, the cost of the electricity when charged on (i) the Domestic tariff and (ii) the Night-rate tariff.

		£
Domestic tariff:	Quarterly charge	7·58
	Units 2000 at 5·01 p	100·20
	Total cost	107·78
Night-rate tariff:	Quarterly charge	10·08
	Day units 1200 at 5·01 p	60·12
	Night units 800 at 1·90 p	15·20
	Total cost	85·40

4. Decorating and Furnishing

The person who intends doing his own home-decorating or furnishing, or the firm providing an estimate for a customer for such a job must first of all decide the quantity of materials required. The more accurately this can be done, the less waste is involved, and the lower the cost of the job.

Example (i) A room 6 metres long by 4·5 metres wide and 2·5 metres high is to be decorated. The ceiling and walls are to have two coats of emulsion paint which has a covering capacity of 14 m² per litre. Allow 12 m² for windows and doors, which are not to be painted. Calculate (i) the total area to be painted and (ii) the cost of the paint at £2·85 per litre. (The smallest-sized tin of paint that can be purchased is a 1-litre tin.)

Area of walls $= 21 \times 2.5$ $= 52.5$
Area of ceiling $= 6 \times 4.5$ $= 27.0$

$$79.5$$
Less: Doors and windows $= 12.0$

$$67.5 \text{ m}^2$$

∴ Area to be painted (2 coats) $= 135 \text{ m}^2$
No. of litres $\dfrac{135}{14} =$ 9.6
∴ No. of litres to buy $= 10$
Cost of paint $= £2.85 \times 10$ $= £28.50$

Example (ii) A carpet is required for a staircase of 18 treads, each of which measures 180 mm high and 260 mm deep. Allow an additional 500 mm for finishing at top and bottom. Estimate the cost of purchasing and fitting the carpet if the carpet costs £6·70 per metre length and there is a fitting charge of 75p per metre. Assume the carpet will be supplied cut to the next 0·5 metre.

Length of carpet required: mm
Treads 18×440 $= 7920$
Finishing $= 500$

Total $= 8420 = 8.420 \text{ m}$

$$\text{Length of carpet to buy} \quad = 8\cdot5 \text{ m}$$

$$\begin{aligned}
\text{Cost of carpet} &= £6\cdot70\times8\cdot5 = £56\cdot95 \\
\text{Fitting charge} &= £0\cdot75\times8\cdot5 = 6\cdot37\tfrac{1}{2}
\end{aligned}$$

$$\text{Total cost} \qquad\qquad = £63\cdot32\tfrac{1}{2}$$

Example (iii) A window 8 ft wide by 3 ft. 9 in. high is to be curtained, using material of width 48 in. The curtains are to be double the width of the window to allow for folds and an extra 6 in. of material is to be allowed on each curtain for finishing top and bottom. Estimate in yards the amount of material to be purchased.

$$\begin{aligned}
\text{No. of lengths of material required} &= 4 \\
\text{Length of each piece} &= 4 \text{ ft. } 3 \text{ in.} \\
\text{Total length of material required} &= 4 \text{ ft. } 3 \text{ in}\times4 \\
&= 17 \text{ ft.} \\
&= 5\tfrac{2}{3} \text{ yds.} \\
\text{Amount to be purchased} &= 6 \text{ yds.}
\end{aligned}$$

5. Assignments L

1. To calculate the average cost per mile to the nearest 1/10p of running a car for one year – depreciation to be included in the cost.

   Data: (i)   Cost of car £3200.
   (ii)   Assumed value after 1 year £2400.
   (iii) Mileage covered 18 000.
   (iv)   Petrol consumption on average 30 m.p.g.
   (v)   Petrol cost average 184 p per gallon.
   (vi)   Tax £85.
   (vii) Insurance £94·50.
   (viii) Repairs and maintenance £87·50.

2. To calculate the 'average' cost per mile of running a small motor-cycle for 1 year.

Data: (i)   Mileage covered 4500.
      (ii)   Petrol consumption 150 miles per gallon.
     (iii) Petrol cost 182 p per gallon.
     (iv)   Tax £8.
      (v)   Insurance £25.
     (vi)   Repairs and maintenance £21·50.
    (vii)   Ignore depreciation in value of machine.

3. To calculate the cost of gas for one quarter. Use rates given in the text.

Data: (i)   Consumer charged on the Credit tariff.
      (ii)   Previous reading   3469 (100 cu.ft.).
     (iii) Present reading   3594 (100 cu.ft.).
     (iv)   Conversion factor from cu.ft. (in hundreds) to therms multiply by 1·032.

4. To calculate the cost of electricity for one quarter. Use rates given in the text.

Data: (i)   Consumer charged on Night-rate tariff.
      (ii)   No. of units used at night 1024.
     (iii) No. of units used during day 856.

5. To calculate the average monthly cost of gas and electricity taken over a one-year period. Use charges quoted in text.

Data: (i)   Gas charged on Credit tariff.
      (ii)   Consumption of gas:
          First   Quarter – 491 therms.
          Second Quarter – 289 therms.
          Third   Quarter – 190 therms.
          Fourth Quarter –   45 therms.
     (iii) Electricity charged on Domestic tariff.
     (iv)   Consumption of electricity:
          First   Quarter – 2339 units.
          Second Quarter – 1591 units.
          Third   Quarter – 1247 units.
          Fourth Quarter – 1513 units.

6. To calculate the cost of painting ceiling and walls of a room.

Data: (i)   Room measure 6·2 m long by 5·2 m wide by 2·4 m high.

    (ii)   Allow 10 m² for area not to be painted.

    (iii)   Two coats of paint to be used.

    (iv)   Paint has a covering capacity of 15 m² per litre.

    (v)   Paint costs £2·80 per litre.

    (vi)   Smallest sized tin of paint that can be purchased 1 litre.

7.   To calculate cost of carpeting a room.

Data: (i)   Room measures 4·9 m long by 3·8 m wide.

        (ii)   Broadloom carpet 2 m wide to be used.

        (iii)   Carpet to be laid with minimum number of joins.

        (iv)   Carpet can be purchased in units of 0·5 m in length.

        (v)   Cost of carpet £8·65 per m².

M. Housing – rates, rent, mortgages

1. Rates – the General Rate

Rates are levied by a Local Authority to cover the cost of services, such as Education and Libraries, which are provided by the Authority. The total amount required to run these various services is charged to the occupants of property, and the amount each individual pays depends on:

(i) the rateable value of the property.

and (ii) the rate levied.

1.1 Rateable Value (R.V.)

Every property is assessed for rate purposes, the assessment depending on the value of the property. The sum of all the individual assessments gives the total Rateable Value for the Authority.

1.2 The Rate Levied

The Rate Levied depends on the amount the Authority wishes to raise and is calculated as a certain amount per £1 of rateable value.

Example (i) The Rateable Value of a Local Authority is £20 000 000. The Authority estimates it needs to raise £27 200 000 from the General Rate. What will be the rate levied?

Rateable Value   = £20 000 000
Estimated Expenditure = £27 200 000

$$\text{Rate Levied} = \frac{\text{Estimated Expenditure}}{\text{Rateable Value}}$$

$$= \frac{£27\ 200\ 000}{£20\ 000\ 000} = £1\!\cdot\!36$$

$$= 136\text{ p}$$

This would be referred to as a rate of 136 p in the £.

Example   (ii)   A house has a rateable value of £300. If the local rate is 136 p in the £, how much will the occupier of the property have to pay in rates?

Rates payable = R.V. × rate levied

$$= £\frac{300}{1} \times \frac{136}{100} = £408$$

2. The Rate Demand

The statement on p. 107 shows in an abbreviated form the particulars of a rate demand for a typical Local Authority. Not every service is listed, and it will be seen that certain services are provided by the District and others by the County. It will also be noticed that if it were not for Domestic Rate Relief and other Government grants the actual rate payable would be very much higher.

3. The Penny Rate

The published rate demand also shows the estimated product of a 1p rate. In the rate demand shown this is given as £245 000 for the District. Therefore the total R.V. for this District is £24 500 000. The product of a penny rate is a useful guide in determining the effect on the rates of major new items of expenditure.

4. Water Rate

In addition to the general rate, a separate water rate has to be paid to the Local Water Authority. This is also charged according to rateable value.

METROPOLITAN DISTRICT OF BANKSIDE
General Rate – Particulars of Items

Purpose	Estimated product of 1 p rate	District purposes	County purposes
	£ 245 000	p	p
Education		113·07	
Environmental Health		2·62	
Social Services		26·34	
Housing		2·24	16·21
Refuse Collection & Disposal		3·86	2·74
Libraries		5·62	
Town Planning		2·14	1·92
Roads/Transport		10·36	20·02
Parks & Open Spaces		8·10	1·12
Fire Service			6·84
Other Services		14·99	11·96
		189·34	60·81
Deduct:			
Appropriations from balances		3·53	3·35
Govt. Grants		85·53	6·24
		89·06	9·59
		100·28	51·22
			100·28
Deduct:			151·50
Domestic Rate Relief			18·50
Rate required for District & County purposes.			133·00

Example   Calculate the water rate payable for a house with a
R.V. of £320 if the rate levied is 9·50 p in the £.

R.V.   = £320
Water rate levied   = 9·50 p
Water rates payable   = 320 × 9·50 p
                      = £30·40

5.   Rent

Rent for accommodation is usually charged on a weekly or monthly
basis. The landlord may charge a figure inclusive of rates, or he may
exclude the rates in which case it becomes the responsibility of the
tenant to pay these direct.

Example   (i)   A landlord charges a rent of £25·00 a week for a flat
plus an amount to cover the rates. In a year when
the rates amount to £163·28 what will be the inclusive amount charged to the tenant?

                                       £
Weekly rent   =   25·00
Weekly rates   =   3·14 (163·28 ÷ 52)

Rent inclusive of rates =   28·14

Example   (ii)   A man owns a house valued at £15 000. The rates
payable are £210 per year. He estimates the annual
cost of repairs, insurance and other expenses at
£250. For how much per month should he let the
house in order to cover these expenses and give him-
self a return of 6% on the capital value of the
house?

The rent must include: £
          Income to owner = 900 (6% of £15 000)
          Rates   = 210
          Repairs, etc.   = 250

                            1360

$$\text{Monthly rent to be charged} = £\frac{1360}{12}$$

$$= £113 \cdot 30 \text{ (to nearest } 10\text{p)}$$

6. House Purchase – Mortgages

A property may be purchased by arranging a mortgage or loan with a Building Society. The Building Society provides the money for the purchase and the purchaser undertakes to repay the loan over a period of time. In return the Building Society has a legal claim on the property should the loan not be repaid. There are several ways in which mortgages can be arranged.

6.1 Fixed Capital Repayments

In this case an agreed amount of capital is repaid each month together with interest on the amount of the loan outstanding. In this way the actual monthly payments will reduce as the loan is paid off.

Example   A man borrows £5000 at 8% per annum. He agrees to repay £20 each month together with interest on the amount of the loan outstanding at the beginning of the month. Show how his repayments will reduce.

First Month.
Loan outstanding $= £5000$

Interest payable $= £\dfrac{8}{100} \times \dfrac{5000}{1} \times \dfrac{1}{12} = £33 \cdot 33$

Capital repayment $\qquad\qquad\quad = £20 \cdot 00$

Total repayment $\qquad\qquad\quad = £53 \cdot 33$

Second Month.
Loan outstanding $= £4980$

Interest payable $= £\dfrac{8}{100} \times \dfrac{4980}{1} \times \dfrac{1}{12} = £33 \cdot 20$

Capital repayment $\qquad\qquad\quad = £20 \cdot 00$

Total repayment $\qquad\qquad\quad = £53 \cdot 20$

6.2   Fixed Instalment Repayment

The more popular type of mortgage is one where the monthly instalment of capital plus interest remains the same throughout the period of repayment subject, of course, to fluctuation in the rate of interest. In this case the Building Society usually quotes monthly repayments for each £1000 borrowed. (The calculation of these amounts is complex and outside the scope of this book.)

Example   A Building Society quotes the repayments on a mortgage when the rate of interest is 12%, and after allowing for income tax relief, as £8·08 per £1000 per month for 25 years. What will be the monthly repayments on a £10 000 mortgage?

Repayment per £1000   =   £8·08
Repayment on £10 000 = £8·08 × 10   =   £80·80

6.3   Income Tax Relief

Tax relief is normally granted on mortgage interest paid to Building Societies. This relief is allowed for by making an appropriate deduction from the monthly mortgage repayments. In the previous example the monthly repayment, without a deduction for tax relief, would have been £8·75 per £1000 per month. Tax relief is, therefore, an important factor in determining the 'real' cost of a mortgage.

6.4 Combined Mortgage and Life Insurance

This is a popular way of arranging house purchase because it provides a degree of security for the family. A Life Insurance policy for at least the value of that loan is taken out. Interest has to be paid on the loan for the whole period of the mortgage after which the money from the insurance policy liquidates the loan.

Example   A man wishes to borrow £10 000 to buy a house. The interest rate is 12%. The loan is to be covered by a Life Insurance policy taken out for the 25 year period which costs £2·87 per £1000 per month. What will be the gross monthly payments involved?

Life Insurance premium = £2·87 × 10   =   £28·70

$$\text{Loan Interest} = £\frac{12}{100} \times \frac{10\ 000}{1} \times \frac{1}{12} \quad = \quad £100\cdot00$$

Gross monthly payment   =   £128·70

As there will be tax relief on the mortgage interest the cost of repaying the mortgage by this method will be reduced to about £99 per month. This compares with a net monthly cost of £80·80 when repayment is made by fixed instalments.

7.   Assignments M

1. To calculate (i) the rate to be levied and (ii) rates payable on a dwelling house.

   Data: (i)   Product of 1 p rate = £285 000.
          (ii)   Amount to be raised by the rates = £37 620 000.
        (iii)   Rateable value of house = £420.

2. To calculate the cost of the Education service in a Local Authority and to express this as a percentage of the total cost of all services provided by the Authority.

   Data: (i)   Product of 1 p rate = £245 000.
         (ii)   Cost of education 113·05 p in the £.
        (iii)   Cost of all services 190·74 p in the £.

3. To estimate the 'inclusive rent' chargeable for a house on a monthly basis given expenses and return on capital value of house required.

    Data: (i)   Value of house £20 000.
    (ii) Income required net 5% of capital value.
    (iii) Rateable value of house £380.
    (iv) General rate 130 p in the £.
    (v)   Water rate 9·50 p in the £.
    (vi) Repairs, maintenance and other expenses to be charged £350.

4. To calculate the monthly repayments for the first three months of a mortgage being repaid on a 'fixed capital' repayment basis. Calculate 1 month's interest as $\frac{1}{12}$ of a year's interest.

    Data: (i)   Mortgage £10 000.
    (ii) Monthly repayments of capital £100.
    (iii) Interest payable at 9% on loan outstanding at beginning of month.

5. To calculate the monthly repayments on a £20 000 mortgage repayable on a 'fixed-instalment' basis, and the 'net' interest payable over the full period of the mortgage.

    Data: (i)   Repayments £8·08 per month for each £1000 of the mortgage net of tax.
    (ii) Mortgage repayable over 25 years.

6. To calculate the monthly cost of a £15 000 mortgage operated on a combined mortgage/life insurance basis and the net monthly payments after allowing for income tax relief.

    Data: (i)   Mortgage interest payable at 12%.
    (ii) Life Insurance premiums £2·87 per £1000 per month.
    (iii) Income tax relief on the mortgage interest at 30%.

7. To calculate the estimated monthly outgoings on the purchase and upkeep of a house.

    Data: (i)   Monthly mortgage payments £96.
          (ii) Rates at 130 p in the £ on R.V. £390.
          (iii) Water rates payable at 9·5 p in the £.
          (iv) House insurance £60 per year.
          (v)   Estimate for repairs and maintenance £400 per year.

N. Savings and insurance

1. Savings

Most people, at some time or another, will wish to save some money. There are many ways in which this can be done, and the one chosen will depend on individual circumstances. For instance, a person with only small savings may be mainly interested in a safe deposit for the money, and ready access to it when required. A person with much larger savings will be more interested in the rate of interest they will earn. The amount of tax payable on the interest received from savings is also important, as this must be taken into account in determining the net interest received. The following are some of the more popular forms of saving:

1.1 National Savings Bank

This is operated by the Post Office and is essentially for small savers. It pays modest rates of interest. In 1984 these were 3% on small balances and 6% on balances of over £500. No tax is payable on the first £70 of interest earned. Withdrawal of money is easy.

Example   (i)   A boy deposits £100 in a National Savings Bank account and leaves it there for two complete years. Interest at 3% is added at the end of each year. What will be the balance in the account after two years?

$$\begin{array}{lll} & & £ \\ \text{Principal year 1} & = & 100{\cdot}00 \\ \text{Interest year 1} & = & 3{\cdot}00 \ (3\% \text{ of } £100) \\ \hline \text{Principal year 2} & = & 103{\cdot}00 \\ \text{Interest year 2} & = & 3{\cdot}09 \ (3\% \text{ of } £103) \\ \hline \text{Balance after 2 years} & = & 106{\cdot}09 \end{array}$$

Example (ii) A man deposits £2000 in the National Savings Bank for 1 year. He receives interest at 6% on this. The first £70 of interest is tax-free and the remainder of the interest is taxed at 30%.

Calculate (i) his net income.
(ii) the net return on his savings (i.e. net income for 1 year as a percentage of his total savings)

$$\begin{array}{llll} & & & £ \\ \text{Interest} & = & \dfrac{6}{100} \times 2000 & = 120{\cdot}00 \\[2mm] \text{Tax payable} & = & \dfrac{30}{100} \times \dfrac{50}{1} & = 15{\cdot}00 \\[2mm] \hline \text{Net Income} & & & = 105{\cdot}00 \\[2mm] \text{Net Return} & = & \dfrac{105}{2000} \times \dfrac{100}{1}\% & = 5{\cdot}25\% \end{array}$$

1.2 National Savings Certificates

These are issued by the Government and are intended for long-term savings. They earn a good rate of interest and the interest is not taxable. There have been a number of different issues of certificates. The 26th issue certificates cost £25 each unit and each unit increases in value to £37·17 after 5 complete years. This is equivalent to compound interest of 8·25% per year if the certificates are held for the full 5-year period. If the certificates are cashed before the end of the period a slightly lower rate of interest is payable as shown in the following table:

Years after purchase	Value at end of year	Rate of interest for the year
1	£26·53	6·12%
2	£28·41	7·09%
3	£30·73	8·17%
4	£33·61	9·37%
5	£37·17	10·59%

Example A man who holds 4 26th issue national savings certificates cashes them after two years. What rate of simple interest has the investment provided?

$$£$$

Initial cost of certificates = 100·00
Cash value of certificates
after 2 years = 113·64
Interest received = 13·64

Rate of simple interest = $\dfrac{100 \times I}{P \times N}$

where
I = £13·64
P = £100
N = 2 years

$$= \frac{100 \times 13·64}{100 \times 2} = \underline{\underline{6·82\%}}$$

1.3 Building Societies

These are extremely popular for both short term and long term savings. They are also convenient for those who save a fixed amount each month. Rates of interest are usually very good and income tax on the interest is paid by the Society.

Example (i) A saver has deposited in a Building Society account £100, on which interest is paid at 7% net of basic rate tax. What is the equivalent gross rate of interest to the person who pays tax at standard rate of 30%?

Building Society deposit = £100
Net income = £7·00
Tax already deducted = 30%

Equivalent gross income = £7·00 × $\dfrac{100}{70}$ = £$\dfrac{700}{70}$ = $\underline{\underline{£10·00}}$

∴ Gross rate of interest = $\dfrac{10}{100} \times \dfrac{100}{1}\%$ = $\underline{\underline{10\%}}$

Example
(ii)

A man has a balance of £200 in a Building Society account at the beginning of January. He makes a regular saving of £10 on the last day of each calendar month. The Society pays interest at 7·5%, the interest being calculated on a daily basis from the day following each deposit. Calculate the balance in his account after 6 complete months.

Interest payable: £
Jan. on £200 for 31 days = 1·2739
Feb. on £210 for 28 days = 1·2082
Mar. on £220 for 31 days = 1·4013
April on £230 for 30 days = 1·4178
May on £240 for 31 days = 1·5287
June on £250 for 30 days = 1·5410

      8·3709 = £8·37

Plus: Initial deposit   = 200·00

Jul. 1 Balance in Account = £208·37

Example
(iii)

A man has a deposit of £200 in a Building Society account paying 5·5% per annum interest net of income tax, the interest being added each half year. What will be the balance on his account after 1 complete year?

           £
Balance 1st Jan.   = 200·00

Interest at 30 June = 200 $\times \dfrac{7·5}{100} \times 0·5 =$ 7·50

Balance 1st July   = 207·50

Interest at 31 Dec. = 207·50 $\times \dfrac{7·5}{100} \times 0·5 =$ 7·78

Balance 1st Jan.   = 215·28

Note. For ease of calculation the half-yearly interest has been calculated as one-half of a full year's interest. It has not been calculated on the basis of the exact number of days in the half-year.

1.4   Bank Deposit

Bank Deposit accounts are usually used for very short term savings. Rates of interest usually compare unfavourably with other forms of savings, but in preference to maintaining a large balance on a current account which pays no interest it is better to transfer surplus cash into a deposit account. Income tax is payable on deposit account interest.

Example   A man has £100 in a bank deposit account which pays interest at 5% per annum, interest being added half-yearly. Tax is payable on the interest at 30%. What will his net income be from this deposit for one complete year?

$$
\begin{array}{lr}
 & £ \\
\text{1st Jan. Balance in account} & = 100 \cdot 00 \\
\text{30th Jun. Interest} = \dfrac{5}{100} \times \dfrac{100}{1} \times 0 \cdot 5 = & 2 \cdot 50 \\[2mm]
\hline
\text{1st July Balance} & = 102 \cdot 50 \\
\text{31st Dec. Interest} = \dfrac{5}{100} \times \dfrac{102 \cdot 50}{1} \times 0 \cdot 5 = & 2 \cdot 56 \\[2mm]
\hline
 & 105 \cdot 06 \\
\hline\hline
\end{array}
$$

Gross Interest received for year	=	5·06
Less: Tax payable at 30%	=	1·52
Net Interest received	=	£ 3·54

2. Insurance

In many aspects of life there is some element of risk involved which can result in financial loss. Fire or burglary can result in loss of possessions, illness or accident can result in loss of earnings, death can mean the loss of a family income. The purpose of insurance is to alleviate, entirely or in part, the loss which may occur. Insurance is effected by taking out a policy which sets down the conditions of the insurance and the amount of the regular payments, called premiums, which the insured has to make. There are two main categories of insurance which affect most people (i) Life assurance and (ii) Property insurance.

2.1 Life Assurance

The most popular type of policy is an Endowment policy which assures a certain sum of money after a specified number of years. Should the policy holder die before this period of time has elapsed the assured sum will be paid to the next of kin or other nominated beneficiary. Some Life Assurance policies are 'with-profits' policies which means that the sum assured may increase over a period depending on the profits of the insurance company. Life Assurance is therefore a form of savings combined with insurance protection.

2.2 Premium Payable

This will vary according to the age of the person taking out the insurance and the period of the insurance. The following is a typical table of premiums for an Endowment 'with-profits' policy.

Monthly Premiums in £ for each £100 assured					
Age next birthday	**No. of years**				
	10	15	20	25	30
20	0·83	0·58	0·42	0·33	0·27
25	0·83	0·58	0·42	0·33	0·28
30	0·83	0·58	0·43	0·34	0·28
40	0·89	0·59	0·44	0·36	0·30
50	0·91	0·62	0·48	0·41	0·38

Example A man aged 25 next birthday wishes to take out an Endowment with-profits policy for a sum of £1500 payable in 15 years. Calculate the annual premium payable (using the figures in the above table).

Monthly premium $\quad$ = £0·58 per £100
∴ Annual premium = £0·58 × 12 per £100
which $\qquad\quad$ = £0·58 × 12 × 15 per £1500
$\qquad\qquad\qquad$ = £104·40

2.3   Income Tax Relief

On life insurance policies taken out prior to the 1984 Budget there is relief of income tax. In 1984 this was at a rate of 15% of the premiums paid. Tax relief does therefore reduce quite substantially the real cost of life insurance. However, since the 1984 budget tax relief on new life insurance policies has been abolished.

2.4   Property Insurance

The most important categories of property insurance are:

(i)   House insurance
(ii)   Contents of the house
(iii)   Car insurance

In categories (i) and (ii) the premiums payable depend on the value of the property insured and these are usually quoted as an annual figure for each £100 cover.

A comprehensive insurance on a house would cost about 15 p per £100 for the building and 50 p per £100 for the contents. Car insurance is very different. First of all it is a legal requirement for all car users. Secondly, the premiums payable will depend on many factors such as the type of car, the age of the insured, the number of accidents in which the driver has been involved. For car insurance individual quotations from companies need to be obtained.

Example   A man owns a house worth £20 000 and values its contents at £5000. How much would his annual premium be if he is charged 15 p per £100 on the house and 50 p per £100 on the contents.

$$
\begin{array}{lr}
 & £ \\
\text{Premium on building } 200 \times 15 \text{ p} & = \ 30{\cdot}00 \\
\text{Premium on contents } 50 \times 50 \text{ p} & = \ 25{\cdot}00 \\
\hline
\text{Total premium} & = \ 55{\cdot}00 \\
\end{array}
$$

3. Assignments N

1. To calculate (i) gross and net income from savings in a National Savings Bank account (ii) net income as a percentage of original deposit.

   Data: (i)   Deposit of £1500 remaining for 2 complete years.
   (ii) Rate of Interest 6% per annum payable yearly.
   (iii) First £70 of interest each year tax free.
   (iv) Tax on remainder of interest at 30%.

2. To calculate the equivalent gross rate of simple interest payable on 26th issue National Savings certificates.

   Data: (i)   Assume certificates are held for the full 5-year period.
   (ii) Rate of tax payable 30%.

3. To calculate (i) the interest payable on a deposit in a building society (ii) the gross rate of interest calculated on a full year basis.

   Data: (i)   £400 deposited for 1 complete year.
   (ii) Rate of interest 7% net of basic rate tax.
   (iii) Interest added to account half-yearly.
   (iv) Basic rate income tax 30%.
   (v)   No further deposits or withdrawals on the account during the year.
   (vi) Assume the half-yearly interest is exactly one-half of a full year's interest.

4. To calculate the interest received on a building society account over a 6 month period.

   Data: (i)   Balance already in account at 1st Jan. £250.
   (ii) Deposit of £20 added on last day of each month.
   (iii) Rate of interest 7·5% payable from day following each deposit.

5. To compare net return over one year from £200 deposited in (i) N.S.B. (ii) Building Society (iii) Bank Deposit or (iv) from a Loan to a Local Authority.

   Data: (i)   N.S.B. pay 3% – with no tax payable on first £70 interest.

   (ii)   Building Society pays 7·5% net of basic rate tax and adds interest half yearly.

   (iii)   Bank pays 5% interest – interest added half-yearly. All of the interest is taxed at 30%.

   (iv)   Local Authority pays 9·5% per annum interest, payable yearly and subject to tax at 30%.

   (v)   Assume half year's interest in the bank deposit or Building Society account is the same as one-half of a full year's interest.

6. To calculate the annual premium payable on an endowment assurance policy and net cost after allowing for tax relief.

   Data: (i)   Use table of premiums given in text.

   (ii)   Sum to be assured £5000.

   (iii)   Term of policy 20 years.

   (iv)   Age next birthday of person taking out insurance 40 years.

7. To calculate the total premiums payable on an endowment assurance for its full term and the net cost after allowing for tax relief.

   Data: (i)   Use table of premiums given in text.

   (ii)   Endowment policy for £20 000.

   (iii)   Period of policy 25 years.

   (iv)   Age next birthday of insured person 30 years.

8. To calculate the cost of insurance on buildings and contents of a house.

   Data: (i)   Insured value of house £25 000.

   (ii)   Insured value of contents £6500.

   (iii)   Premium on building 15 p per £100.

   (iv)   Premium on contents 50 p per £100.

9. To calculate increase in premiums on a house and its contents.

Data: (i) Present insurance on house £20 000 at 12·5 p per £100.
  (ii) Present insurance on contents £3000 at 30 p per £100.
  (iii) Revised value of house £25 000.
  (iv) Revised value of contents £5000.
  (v) Revised premium rates 15 p per £100 on house and 50 p per £100 on contents.

Answers

Exercise A1

1. £101 541
2. −57·9 Therms
   +£16·44
3. Profit £32·38

4. £2853·32
5. £88·39
6. £108·86

Exercise A2

1. 1764
2. 192 087
3. 18 600
4. 118 604
5. 2 249 100

6. 70 500
7. 12 524
8. 74 481
9. 71 179
10. 40 320

Exercise A3

1. 353
2. 324 Rem. 16
3. 35
4. 56
5. 2830

6. 219 Rem. 26
7. 49 Rem. 63
8. 32
9. 57   Rem. 57
10. 2   Rem. 270

Exercise A4

1. 3^4
2. $3^2 \times 11$
3. $2^2 \times 31$
4. $3^2 \times 41$

5. $2^5 \times 3 \times 5$
6. $3^3 \times 19$
7. $2^2 \times 3^3 \times 41$
8. $2^3 \times 3 \times 5^2 \times 7 \times 19$

9. 6
10. 15
11. 14
12. 19
13. 18
14. 30

15. 40
16. 240
17. 240
18. 180
19. 144
20. 960

Exercise A5

1. $6\frac{11}{16}$
2. $9\frac{2}{5}$
3. $5\frac{41}{48}$
4. $4\frac{5}{8}$
5. $2\frac{11}{12}$
6. $2\frac{7}{10}$
7. $6\frac{1}{8}$
8. $7\frac{5}{16}$

9. $14\frac{7}{8}$
10. $3\frac{3}{10}$
11. $3\frac{7}{13}$
12. $2\frac{13}{14}$
13. $1\frac{1}{12}$
14. $6\frac{1}{2}$
15. $1\frac{1}{32}$
16. $7\frac{2}{3}$

Exercise A6

1. (i) $6\frac{4}{5}$
   (ii) $3\frac{16}{25}$
   (iii) $\frac{7}{8}$
   (iv) $\frac{3}{400}$
   (v) $1\frac{463}{500}$
2. (i) 0·0625
   (ii) 0·35
   (iii) 0·416
   (iv) 0·09
   (v) 0·26
3. (i) 2·47
   (ii) 3·4
   (iii) 0·068
   (iv) 4·59
   (v) 7·360
   (vi) 6·00
4. 25·953
5. 19·94

6. 3·27
7. 4·55
8. 10·315
9. 426·5
10. 32
11. 24 500
12. 56·32
13. 0·1692
14. 0·001 53
15. 7·392
16. 18·384
17. 0·000 105
18. 62
19. 3·1
20. 45
21. 0·4
22. 4
23. 2·5

Test Paper A

1. £12·29
2. 10 830·4 (1 d.p.)
3. 11 600
4. 16·5
5. 4·0
6. £22·10
7. 0·016
8. $8\frac{29}{32}$
9. $10\frac{3}{4}$
10. $4\frac{1}{4}$

11. 1·756
12. $2^3 \times 3^2 \times 5 \times 7$
13. 120
14. 4
15. 0·1875
16. 18/25
17. £93
18. £0·31
19. £145·16
20. £1525·05

Exercise B1

1. £5·06
2. £40·50
3. (i) 2·468
   (ii) 1·27
   (iii) 12 000
4. 68p

5. £92·25
6. £6·35
7. £1·24
8. £688·94
9. £22·14
10. 49·4 km

Exercise B2

1. £25·35
2. 531·90 francs. 13 320 pesetas
3. 54 p (nearest p)
4. £741 (nearest £)
5. £183·42

Exercise B3

1. (i) 112 cm²
   (ii) 2500 cm²
   (iii) 20 088 cm²
   (iv) 207 km²
2.   1·014 m²

3. 3·5 m
4. 41·760 m²
5. 24·15 m²
6. 53 m²
7. 9 hectares

Test Paper B

1. 2·468 m
2. 3465 g
3. 7·256 hectares
4. 49·5 litres
5. £261·80
6. £20·88
7. 15 p
8. 3568 pesetas
9. £31·56
10. 40·48 p

11. 16·56 m²
12. 49·5 m²
13. 26·1048 hectares
14. 47
15. 43 km.p.h. (nearest whole no.)
16. 1707 (nearest whole no.)
17. £257·93
18. 25 kg
19. 48 km/hr.
20. 17 tonnes

Test Paper C

1.   (i) 2440
  (ii) 47 900
  (iii) 0·006
  (iv) 49 600
  (v) 0·45
  (vi) 0·070
  (vii) 12·0
  (viii) 12·006
  (ix) 15·74
  (x) 15·74

2.   (i) 61·93
  (ii) 0·75
  (iii) 189·84
  (iv) 0·0021
  (v) 0·0021
  (vi) 410
  (vii) 0·0034
  (viii) 624·8
  (ix) 0·050
  (x) 0·01
  (xi) 131·2
  (xii) 48·53

Exercise D1

1.   (i) 20%
  (ii) 25%
  (iii) $33\frac{1}{3}$%
  (iv) 18·75%
  (v) 112·5%
2.   (i) 50%
  (ii) 34%
  (iii) 17·5%
  (iv) 0·5%
  (v) 185%

3.   (i) $\frac{3}{20}$
  (ii) $\frac{3}{8}$
  (iii) $1\frac{2}{5}$
  (iv) $\frac{2}{3}$
  (v) $\frac{4}{5}$
4.   (i) 0·4
  (ii) 0·0375
  (iii) 0·275
  (iv) 2·5
  (v) 0·005

5.   (i)   £3·60
    (ii)   £0·63
    (iii) £15·63 (nearest penny)
    (iv) 0·61
    (v)   0·10p (nearest penny)
    (vi) 292
    (vii) 26·25 kg
    (viii) 0·085 litres
    (ix) 0·63 metres
    (x)   18 140

6.   (i)   £72
    (ii)   £150
    (iii) £4·50
    (iv) 350 kg
7.   (i)   37·5%
    (ii)   8%
    (iii) 25·9% (1 d.p.)
    (iv) 5·3% (1 d.p.)
8.   £157·03 (nearest penny)
9.   9·6%
10.   7·5% (1 d.p.)

Exercise D2

1.   (i)   £3·60
    (ii)   £5·51 (nearest penny)
    (iii) 64·5 p
    (iv) £14
    (v)   £2·08
    (vi) 12·5%
    (vii) 14·3% (1 d.p.)

2.   (i)   40 p
    (ii)   £12·81
    (iii) £4·80
    (iv) £8·17
    (v)   £28
    (vi) Profit 17·5%
    (vii) Loss 24%

Exercise D3

1.   (i)   I = £150, A = £1150
    (ii)   I = £1·64, A = £121·64
    (iii) A = £2420, T = 6 yrs.
    (iv) I = £18·36, T = 292 days
    (v)   A = £7504·40, R = $3\frac{1}{2}$%
    (vi) P = £756, A = £1005·48

2.   £96
3.   20%
4.   297 francs
5.   £410·52

Exercise D4

1.   (i)   £96
    (ii)   £195
    (iii) £746
    (iv) £271
2.   £393·56
3.   £664·30

4.   (i)   £562·43
    (ii)   £1808·78
    (iii) £3359·80
    (iv) £1379·76
5.   £34 791 (nearest £)

Test Paper D

1.	(i)	62·5%	9.	£148·75
	(ii)	4·5%	10.	£37·22
2.	(i)	0·27	11.	7·75%
	(ii)	0·725	12.	£1660
3.		£4·34	13.	£143
4.		33·3%	14.	£1000
5.		24%	15.	£6029 (nearest £)
6.		£2·72		
7.		£2·53		
8.		£2·59 (nearest penny)		

Test Paper E

1.		£587	9.	(i)	68·08
2.		£180·34		(ii)	75
3.	(i)	£29	10.	(i)	£7500
	(ii)	67·5		(ii)	£9170
	(iii)	63·6		(iii)	£8133 (nearest £)
4.		45	11.	(i)	41
5.		9		(ii)	55
6.	(i)	£249·47½		(iii)	43
	(ii)	12 972·70		(iv)	26
7.		£2853	12.		£2400
8.		7 km/h			

Test Paper F

7.	(i)	18·9°
	(ii)	11·24, 14·48

Assignments G

1. Balance £328·81
2. Balance £441·70
4. Balance £7·71

Assignments H

1. Gross pay £148·40
   Net pay   £117·74
2. Gross pay £605
   Net pay   £442·94
3.   Gross   N.I.
   (i)   £48·25   £4·34
   (ii) £63·15   £5·68
   (iii) £68·00   £6·12
   (iv) £75·50   £6·80

4. (i) Gross   £528·54
         Net   £428·47
      (ii) 81·1%   (1 d.p.)
5.   Gross   Net
   A   £69·00   £52·39
   B   £54·00   £42·66
   C   £49·50   £38·72
   D   £56·68   £48·43
   E   £38·70   £35·22

Assignments I

1.   £104·38
2. (i)   £22·70
   (ii) 20·64%
3. (i)   £115·75
   (ii) 18·37%

4. Code 290
5. £117·30 (tables)
   £117·38 (calculated)

Assignments J

1.   £103·59
2. (i)   £5·86
   (ii)   £1·66
   (iii) £1·17
   (iv)   £1·86
   (v)   £1·79
3. (i)   £43·51
   (ii)   £18·63
   (iii) £66·24
   (iv)   £379·50
4. A   £1·09
   B   £1·23
   C   £0·98
   D   £0·40
   E   £0·84

5. (i)   £60·78
   (ii)   £107·44
   (iii) £14·41
   (iv)   £20·83
   (v)   £18·11
6.   Gross £1193
          Net £282

Assignments K

1. (i) £13·75
   (ii) 24·32%
2. £3·41
3. (i) 16·94%
   (ii) 30·5%

4. (i) 10%
   (ii) 18·95%
5. 38·4%

Assignments L

1. 12·1 p
2. 2·4 p
3. £53·12
4. £72·43

5. £62·09
6. £30·80
7. £173

Assignments M

1. (i) 132 p
   (ii) £554·40
2. (i) £27 697 250
   (ii) 59·27%
3. £157 (nearest £)
4. (i) £175
   (ii) £174·81
   (iii) £174·62

5. £161·60
   £28 480
6. Gross £193·05
   Net £148·05
7. £179·67

Assignments N

1. (i) Gross £185·40
      Net £171·78
   (ii) 11·45% over 2 years
2. 13·91% Simple Interest
3. (i) £28·49
   (ii) 10·18%
4. £11·16
5. (i) N.S.B. £6
   (ii) Bldg. Soc. £15·28
   (iii) Bank £7
   (iv) Local Authority £13·30

6. £264
7. £20 400
8. £70
9. £28·50